Tempus ORAL HISTORY *Series*

voices of
Dukinfield and Stalybridge

Tempus ORAL HISTORY *Series*

voices of
Dukinfield and Stalybridge

Derek J. Southall

TEMPUS

Leaving Dukinfield on Oxford Road, as it goes down into High Street, Stalybridge.

Frontispiece: *Leaving Dukinfield (then part of Cheshire) for Ashton-under-Lyne (then part of Lancashire). Asda now stands where the building on the right is.*

First published 2003

Tempus Publishing Limited
The Mill, Brimscombe Port,
Stroud, Gloucestershire, GL5 2QG

British Library Cataloguing in Publication Data.
A catalogue record for this book is available from the British Library.

ISBN 0 7524 2679 6

Typesetting and origination by Tempus Publishing Limited
Printed in Great Britain by Midway Colour Print, Wiltshire

Contents

Melbourne Street, Stalybridge, flooded in May 1906.

It is with sadness that I record that Mr David Cooper, Mr Percy Norton and Miss Lily Birch have died since I conducted the interviews for this book.

Acknowledgements

I would like to record my thanks to those whose words and photographs make up this book for the generous and unstinting way in which they responded to my requests for interviews and pictures. They are: Mrs Ethel Anderson, Miss Lily Birch, Mrs Pat Bolt, Mr David Cooper, Mr Alex Cox, Mrs Alice Edwards, Mr Tom Evans, Mrs Ethel Gee, Mr Kenneth Gee, Mrs Lily Gover, Mrs Margaret Green, Mrs Joyce Hall, Mrs Gladys Heap, Mrs Vera Win Hotchkiss, Mrs Nellie Howarth, Mrs Betty Jones, Mr David Jones, Mrs Edith Jones, Mrs Barbara Lea, Mr Percy Norton, Mrs Barbara Perry, Mr John Perry, Mrs Jean Pilling, Mrs Nellie Preston, Mrs May Redford, Miss Annice Ritson, Mr Bob Sleigh, Mr Fred Travis, Mrs Joyce Travis, Mr James Wainwright, Mr Ron Watkins, Mrs Evelyn Whitworth and Mrs Alice Young.

My sincere thanks also to Alice Lock and the staff of the Local Studies Library in Stalybridge for their patience and the invaluable help they gave me in my efforts to find some of the photographs included in the book and for permission to reproduce them.

Introduction

In the autumn of 2000, my book, *Voices of Ashton-under-Lyne*, – an oral history of the town in which I have lived for forty years – was published. It was well received, and it was that which prompted me to write this new compilation about Ashton-under-Lyne's immediate neighbours, Dukinfield and Stalybridge.

The two volumes belong to the genre termed oral history, and it is important that the reader understands from the outset what exactly is meant by this.

When we think of the discipline of history, we think of carefully researched facts, backed up by extensive and painstaking research, enabling the accepted establishing of those facts. Oral history, too, gathers together facts about the past, but there the similarity ends. The facts presented as oral history are the facts stored in the memories of people who lived the events and times. Memory, as we all know, is an imperfect thing. We all like to think that our memories are crystal clear, and that things occurred exactly as we remember them. Quite the reverse is true. We may believe that we have a flawless recall of the past; in actual fact our memories are imperfect. While the gist of a well-known event or incident or a personal experience is easy enough to recall, specific facts related to those things may not be as easily remembered or may be recollected imprecisely. So, if you are looking for solid, accurate historical fact, you may not find it in oral history. If, on the other hand, you are looking for information about what it was like to live in a particular place at a particular time, for the personal slant of the memories recollected by the people who lived in that place at that time, then oral history is the answer. In oral history you will find the joy, the sadness, the high and the low spots, family and public events, all seen through the eyes of the people who lived them. You will also see, through those same memories, the way things used to look; the streets and buildings, some long vanished, and the towns in which they lived and of which they speak, always with affection and often very movingly.

This oral history of Dukinfield and Stalybridge during the first half of the twentieth century is an attempt to create a picture of life in these two towns which were, until the boundary changes of 1972, in the north-east corner of Cheshire, close to its border with Lancashire. Since 1972 they have been two of the nine towns which make up the Metropolitan Borough of Tameside, which, in its turn, is part of Greater Manchester.

The book has been compiled from tape-recorded interviews, which I conducted over a period of some twelve months or so with more than thirty people who were born in Dukinfield or Stalybridge in the first half of the last century. Many of those whom I interviewed were in their eighties or nineties and have lived in Dukinfield or Stalybridge all their lives. In order to conduct the interviews I visited them in their homes, and I would like to put on record my gratitude to every one of the interviewees for the warm welcome they gave me, and the frankness and friendliness with which they answered my questions. When I had the recorded interviews, I transcribed each one (the hardest and most laborious part of compiling the book). Then, from the transcriptions, I selected those parts of the interviews which I felt best fitted my purpose; it is those which I have used to compile my book.

The interviewing was the most pleasurable part of the work. Those whom I interviewed spoke freely, and what they had to say was invariably quite fascinating. Every one of those interviewed began by telling me that they were pleased to talk to me but didn't think they had anything interesting to tell me. Then, for an hour or so, they proceeded to tell me things which I found were quite riveting. Often, it would only be the ninety-minute tape running out that brought an interview to its conclusion. I would like to thank all those whom I interviewed for welcoming me into their homes and for being willing to talk about their lives and to share with me, and ultimately with a much wider audience, their memories, even those that were sad and sometimes painful.

The memories of the Dukinfield and Stalybridge people recounted throughout this book are illustrated by many personal photographs. By far the majority of these were loaned to me by the interviewees, who kindly gave me permission to use them in the book. Oral history needs the personal touch to make it come alive, and that personal touch is to be seen most vividly in the photographs. I am most grateful to everyone who loaned me their photographs. I know how precious they are and how much they mean to you all.

It is my hope that the picture of Dukinfield and Stalybridge that emerges in the pages of my book is a true reflection of the time to which it relates, as well as being an accurate transcription of what was told to me. I have tried throughout to use only the words used by the interviewees, since I believe that it is of the greatest importance to be true to what they said. A word or two has occasionally been inserted by me for the sake of clarity.

Compiling this book was a great pleasure for me. I came to the north west in 1959 to take up a teaching post. That teaching post was at Astley County Grammar school for Girls on Yew Tree Lane in Dukinfield, and I spent the whole of my teaching career, all twenty-nine years of it, at the school. I had the privilege of teaching many girls, and eventually boys also, from Dukinfield, and from its neighbour Stalybridge, young people, many of whom have gone on to reflect great credit on their communities. So I feel I have a link with the two towns and their people, whom I have always found to be down to earth, warm and friendly. I would like to think that my book is a fitting tribute to Dukinfield and Stalybridge and their people.

I should like to dedicate *Voices of Dukinfield and Stalybridge* to all the young people of the two towns whom it was my great privilege to know and to teach at Astley from 1959 to 1988.

1 Childhood

Childhood fun and games

We played hopscotch; we had to draw it with chalk on the pavement like the shape of an aeroplane. Hop, hop, hop, all these squares, No. 1, No. 2 – we used to do that, and we used to play like baseball, running around. And skipping ropes. Dad worked at the mill at the back, Chadwick's, for a while. They had big barrels; I don't know what was in them. They had a wire, like a hoop, around the top.

Well, in them days you used to run with a hoop, then you'd catch it. I kept wanting one of these and Dad said, 'Look, if there's one, I'll get one.' So eventually I did get one. Went all round our block; thought it were marvellous. Dad used to say, 'You can't bring that indoors', so it had to go in the coal shed. Then he bought me a bike, a two-wheeled bike, a biggish one. Me brother'd have a ride; he were two years older than me. I'd stand on the back. Sometimes we were very naughty. We'd

Betty Taylor (Mrs Betty Jones) and friends in the garden of her house in Tame Valley. Chadwick's Mill is in the background.

knock on the doors and run away. One day me friend from next door but one was running round in the dark, and this hand come and grabbed her. She couldn't stop crying. Her mum said, 'You're not going out playing any more.' I said, 'It's not me,' but it were, y'know.

Mrs Betty Jones

Bringing in the cows

When I were younger we moved to the Brushes. It was just like a cottage. Me dad thought he'd try and make a bit of money and he bought three cows. When I used to get home from school, that were my job, to go and get the cows in. When it were foggy, you didn't know where cows were that were in t'wood. So I used to have to go and stop and keep listening if I could hear these cows, and, when I found 'em, I used to take 'em back into the shed and tie them up, while me dad come, ready for milking. He even learned me how to do milking. Me mother said she'd never learn. 'You can be too clever,' she said, 'When you can't do it, y'know he's coming home at night.'

Mrs Margaret Green

By bike up the Brushes Estate

As a little lad I had to get a job. Everybody had a job; you were either a paperboy, or a butcher's rounds' lad. I got this job at Ainsworth's in Stalybridge; it was on what they called the Mount, which was higher up than where the old town hall used to be. I used to have to deliver all sorts of things on

Brushes Cottage and the wood where Margaret Mason (Mrs Margaret Green) looked for the cows.

this butcher's bike, with a great big trailer. It weighed a ton, and I was only slightly built. I used to have to peddle this bloody bike up to the Brushes Estate, up that flaming hill, in the middle of winter, in all conditions. I used to finish up wet through. I'd be delivering these big boxes of groceries and I'd feel like a drowned rat when I got up there. It was great coming back, 'cos it was all downhill. I'd finish school at four o'clock and go straight there, and finish about eight o'clock at night. I got half a crown a week for that, which was a lot of money at that time.

Mr Ron Watkins

Harry's canal adventure

There were so many children. It was safe to play out. You had no fear. I mean, we used to go down to the river and paddle in the water, without our parents knowing. And walk down the canal side quite often; it was regular for us to go and look at the canal. I always remember running our Harry down the slope. He was in a trolley, y'know, when he was little, and we were running down [the canal side] and we couldn't stop. Of course, the trolley went into the water, and Harry sat with his feet in the water. All the children were holding on to the handle until two men across the way came across the bridge and saw us and pulled it up.

Miss Annice Ritson

Sharing out the toffees

We didn't have pocket money because there were nine of us children. On Friday night we had to sit in a row on the sofa. Mother used to buy a quarter of toffees or half a pound and they went so far around the nine of us – then, when all the toffees had been given out, the following week my mum started with which-

ever one of us would have been next to have one. But she always saw that we had collection on a Sunday. We always had to go to Sunday school and we always had a penny collection.

Mrs Alice Young

Object of envy

There was a girl who lived in the next block to us. She was an only one. After tea she'd come out eating a brown-bread sandwich. We never had brown bread. I used to look at that sandwich very longingly. As a child I went to dancing school; it was down near County Bridge – there was a little sweet shop there and upstairs it was a dancing school, run by two sisters, Elsie and Doris Hurst. I was having a costume made one day; one of the neighbours was making it for me. I remember turning round on the table, as the neighbour pinned up the hem of my dress, and a lady who was standing there, a very tall, thin lady, said, 'Who's this little bit of importance, then?'

Mrs Alice Edwards

Hard lessons learned

My dad worked at home; he had a shoe-menders at the top of Castle Hall. He was always there. You don't realize it when you're little, but my dad was very wise. If he advised me not to do something and I did it, then it was on my head. One of my earliest memories – I'd only be about four – I had this black doll, which I was very attached to. I'm going out with it through the shop and he said, 'You're not taking that doll out, I hope, and going to play with those Lewis girls.' I said 'Yes. Why?' 'You take that out, lady and they'll break it for you. Within a quarter of an hour you'll be in here in tears. Don't come running to me.' I don't think it lasted ten minutes; its head was all smashed. I ran in. He didn't come. Carried

Jean Travis (Mrs Jean Pilling) aged four.

on mending his shoes. We had a wall outside. He used to say, 'One of these days, lady, you'll fall off that wall. Don't come running in here when you're covered with blood, 'cos I shan't see to you.' 'Course it happened. Teeth through my lip. I've still got the mark. My mother was upset, but he didn't budge. You think they're hard at the time, but that was how you learned, wasn't it.

Mrs Jean Pilling

Getting round my dad

My dad had a workshop, sheet metal works. It were a prominent place in Stalybridge at that time. When I were going to school many a time, if I wanted anything, I knew I couldn't get it off my mother; she hadn't the money. I'd go up to my father and I'd always get it. He always grumbled. I remember going to his

Jean Travis' mother's family outside 62 Kay Street.

Mr John Birch, Miss Lily Birch's father, with his dog, Rex.

workshop from school. I couldn't reach the latch to open the big door. The lads put a box for me to climb on, and I can remember just being able to open the door catch. Sometimes, when I got there, one of the fellows would pull a face, as much as to say, 'Your father's not in a good mood. I wouldn't go in'. I'd go and sit on a pot of paint. I can see myself now.

Miss Lily Birch

Tea with Uncle John

We were living then in St Mark's Street, near the church. There were an explosion the other side of the canal. We got the full effect of the blast. We'd no doors, no windows, no anything; they'd all gone. My mother said we had to go to the top of Chapel Hill, near where the war memorial is. We'd all have to go up there, near where the air will be cleaner and we could get out of this smell. Now I'm a Methodist, with all that that means. My

uncle John had a shop on Town Lane, but, horror of horrors, it was an off-licence. Uncle John gave us tea that day. It's the only time I'd seen him; the only time we'd anything to do with him; but he gave us tea that day and something to eat.

Mr David Cooper

My first doll

We always had Christmas. Always had a Christmas tree. Sometimes we had a rabbit, or a chicken. Or, if my mam were a bit flush, we had a shank of pork. Never had a goose or a turkey. We couldn't go out at Christmas; we had to be at home. I remember, when I was little, we never had anything hardly; they bought me a doll. First doll I ever had. And my brother broke it before we got up on Christmas morning. The only doll I ever had.

Mrs May Redford

The Cooper children, c. 1920. Back: Leslie and David; front: James and Harriet.

Looking after my dolls

When I was six we moved up to Pickford Lane. We had a big back, a big garden type of thing. They used to have a communal wash house in this back. When my mother were washing, my brother Frank used to put me a little line up between trees, and I used to be washing and hanging my dolls' clothes up, y'know. There used to be a man called Mr Marsden, who had a little toffee shop. I used to always be sat on their step, talking to the dolls.

Mrs Ethel Gee

Childhood finances

As I got older and we moved to Railway Street, I used to go errands for the lady next door – a lot of errands, not just one a day – every day for 4d a week. When I was eleven I went to Lakes Road school. There was a trip from the school to London. Not being very well off in the family, I asked if I could put my 4d a week towards the trip to London, which my mother let me do. So I went to London. Other than that I used to give her the 4d a week – it contributed to the family finances. We didn't get pocket money. But, when my father was in work, we used to get a Friday penny. We used to buy sweets, two halfpenny worth.

Mrs Alice Edwards

May Goddard (Mrs May Redford) aged one, front left.

Making the money stretch

In 1938-39 I was getting sixpence a week spending money. I could go to the pictures for 2d; I could buy the 2d Beano or Dandy and I could have a 2d Rolo. Those were the prices then.

Mr Tom Evans

Caught in the act

There used to be a timber yard lower down Peel Street, called Storr's Timber. The office was on one side and a small yard, and on the other side they had what they called the big store yard, where they kept the wood stored. In Duke Street there was a smallish wall, what we could climb up, and we used to go in and play among the timber. One evening I was getting back over the wall. All of a sudden I felt a big hand in the middle of my back. He tanned my backside and then, when he lifted me down, I saw it were the flipping policeman. He turned round and he said, 'You won't be going in there again, will you?' 'No, mister,' I said. 'Right, then. Off you go.' When you saw a copper, you went the opposite way – always. In them days they were all six foot six and built like man-mountains. You never argued with a policeman in them days because you knew you'd come off worse. I never forgot that – he pinned me to the wall with one hand and dusted my backside with the other.

Mr Bob Sleigh

How to make a cricket ball

I was very keen on sport and we used to play cricket. When we were young you couldn't afford to buy cricket balls, so my mother used to start with a little piece of cork, and then she would wrap cotton round it. She would spend hours wrapping cotton around and tying it,

Amelia, John Perry's mum, in the backyard of their house in Tame Valley.

until you finished up with a ball, a ball of cotton or string. I was very popular because I had a ball. I used to take my ball out, somebody else took a bat and we used a lamp-post a lot of times for the wicket. Or you'd go in the bottom of the cemetery and play your cricket there or the Butcher's Field, Bowker and Balls' Field. The ball would eventually start to get smaller and smaller, as the string started to come off. Then you'd have to cut it or snap it off until you finished with a very small ball. Then you'd get a new one from your mother when she'd wrapped it. If you lost the ball, you'd spend hours and hours looking for it.

Mr John Perry

Tom and the three trams

When I was two we went up Huddersfield Road, opposite the Reindeer pub, and we lived there till I was nine. For a child that was absolute heaven. There was no Copley Comprehensive School, no sports stadium, no Copley estate, just the hen pens, pigsties and gardens. I could play in the fields in absolute safety. My dad used to come to the back gate and just put his fingers in his mouth and give a whistle and Tom would come running home. When he was working, my mother would let me play out on these fields. Trams used to go up Huddersfield Road in those days to Upper Mossley, to Ashton, down through Heyheads, down Huddersfield Road, past the town hall and on to St Michael's Square in Ashton. When it came five o'clock it was the start of three trams – five o'clock, five past five and the third tram came at ten past five. On the third tram up, the ten past five, I had to go in, to be ready for my father coming home from Copley mill at quarter past five.

Mr Tom Evans

Snow and fireworks in the Big Back

We used to play on Mary Street and in the Big Back. Everybody played together in them days; there were a lot of children around. It were on a slant, y'know. I can remember winter when it snowed. We used to all have sledges and we used to come down that Big Back and bang right into Hinchliffe's. On 5 November we had big bonfires in the Big Back. It were organized. I didn't like fireworks; I were scared of bangers. My mother used to take me to Princess out of the way.

Mrs Nellie Preston

Cold water surprise

At 5 November, when it was bonfires, we used to have a bonfire in our back and next year they had it in next back. They used to make roast potatoes and parkin and all sorts, and all children used to come. They used to raid then for wood; they used to go raiding and we used to keep it in the backyard. Sometimes they'd climb over our backyard and pinch it. So they used to put a bath of cold water at the back gate. I don't know whether anybody ever fell in.

Mrs Ethel Gee

Sleeping with the dead

We once lived at Belgrave House, on Ashton Road, Denton. We had a lodger who was about eighty. He died while he was living with us. Those days they used to lay them out and leave them in the house. His body was in the next bedroom to my brother and myself. We were left in this house; we were always on our own at night. The bathroom was down a passage and we always used to bath together (we were six and eight). We came out of the bathroom this particular night and I said, 'Ooh, I've heard something.' We had an alarm clock with big bells on the top. One of us had that, the other had a pair of scissors. We had to come down this passage till we got to our bedroom. We were petrified. Three or four nights he was laid out in that room next door – it wasn't a nice experience.

Mrs Joyce Travis

Playing with the dead

We used to play in the cemetery. We used to make dens in the rhododendron bushes and what-have-you in the cemetery. The cemetery and the river separated Tame Valley from the rest of Dukinfield. One part of the cemetery, near the Rock Terrace, there was a wall going up – they used to say if ever you went over that wall something terrible would happen to you. We had this long rope; we used to put these long ropes on the trees and swing on them. You used to go over this wall, and we used to sing, 'She flies through the air'. There was a girl called Sylvia Ash. I remember her on the rope and when it came back she wasn't on the end of it. We were sure that something terrible must have happened to her.

Mrs Barbara Perry

Something a child shouldn't see

Going to Hyde in those days, you went over Hough Hill, along Wood Road and came out at the Rising Moon on Matley Lane. Then you were in Newton. Going that way, you went through the Castle Hall area of Stalybridge. In those days the labour exchange was up there. I remember passing the place with my dad, on that walk to Hyde. There was a queue. I don't know how long, but it was a long queue, two or three deep. As we passed somebody out of that queue shouted to my dad, 'Eh, Wilf! You shouldn't bring a child past these sorts of places.'

Mr Tom Evans

'Run with aunties' dinners'

My mother was one of ten. Three of her sisters worked in various mills in Tame Valley, one in Tower Mill, two in Park Road mill. We used to take their dinners for them at dinnertime. We used to come out of school and run down to Tame Valley with their dinners to the mill.

Miss Annice Ritson

Delivering the dinners

Down Tame Valley there was a very good confectioner's, Rawson's. It was right across from our house, and it was a mixed business as well. Mum used to shop there and they were friends of hers. When I was on holiday from school, they used to say, 'Would you like to take me a few dinners to the mill?' She took a big, strong basket, and she put them in, put a paper over the top so that nothing could get in them, and I used to take them. She used to make them in little pudding basins; some would have hotpot, some would have potato pie, they were all different. She always bought me a pair of what she called moccasins for Christmas, lovely slippers with fur and beads on.

Mrs Betty Jones

Auntie Alice's pea soup

Everybody mucked in together, joined in with everything. When it were bonfire night, there were this square where we lived and we used to have a big bonfire in the centre of it. Everybody that had anything to burn, it went on the bonfire. We had roast potatoes and we had pea soup. My auntie Alice was great at making pea soup – that was one of the best things she could ever make. She used to make it for the Salvation Army.

Mr Bob Sleigh

That was the King, that was!

I remember going to school for the first day, when I was five, to Crescent Road Junior School. I didn't like it really, leaving me mother. When it was the Coronation, in 1937, they said, 'The King's going to pass.' We came out of school onto Wellington Street.

Old Chapel musical production, to celebrate the Coronation of King George VI in 1937.

We were stood outside the school and this car passed at the bottom of Wellington Street. They said, 'Oh, there's the king.' The car passed a few hundred yards away. I didn't even know it were the King until somebody said.

Mr Kenneth Gee

Marching with the Salvation Army

When the Salvation Army came, they used to come with sort of concertina bands, teaching us little songs, religious little songs or little marching songs. They used to have us marching around singing. They'd give you a pencil if you remembered these songs. They'd have all the children lined up and they'd march us to St Mark's, where they had taken a room. They used to ask, would anybody come to be saved? When my mother found out, she said, 'Why didn't you tell them you were Church of England?' But we thought it was wonderful, singing these songs and marching down the street.

Mrs Nellie Preston

Spending money

I used to go to Sunday school and I used to have 3d when I were little, three pennies. One were for collection at the morning; one were for collection at Sunday school in the afternoon; one were for night at church. That were my spending money!

Mrs Ethel Gee

Bonfire Night

We had our own little gang. In those seven houses on Robinson Street there must have been twenty kids. Harry Bostock was the oldest; he was two years older than me.

On Bonfire night mum used to find the meat, Mrs Saville'd find the potatoes, somebody else gave us the pastry and Mr Sykes made a huge potato pie; somebody else gave the peas. A lady who lived on High Street, but whose back door came to our back yard, made treacle toffee and parkin. We used to have fireworks we'd gone round with the guy for. We just went round and knocked on the doors. We used to say, 'A bit of coal to put on the fire.' One lady came to the door and said, 'I'm sorry. I've no coal. Will 2d do?' Would it! It bought two fireworks.

Mrs Ethel Anderson

Change for the Minder's Arms

There was a great spirit in Tame Valley. Camaraderie. You never had to lock your doors. People would just knock, announce themselves and walk in. Everybody knew everybody. The SHMD bus depot was down there. That brings back memories of me going to the bus depot for change for the public house, the Minder's Arms. It was just further up from where I lived and that's how I got my pocket money. She'd give me so much money (I can't remember the landlady's name) and I would take it to the bus depot and get some change and then bring it back. My mother always used to like a drink of beer, but she wouldn't go in a public house. So she had a jug, which I took along to the pub and which was filled up with beer and which I then brought back to the house.

Mr John Perry

The horse 'n' cart

When we lived up Beezum Lane, if we wanted coal, my dad used to have to get the horse 'n' cart and go to Hardy's in Stalybridge, and get coal and bring it back home. I used to have to watch for him coming, on what they called Middle Banking, and have the other

Duke and Percy belonged to Margaret Mason's (Mrs Margaret Green's) dad. They went missing in the 1947 snow.

horse ready, because, as the lane went up, it was very steep, and it was too much for one horse to pull. There'd probably be more than a ton of coal in the cart. I used to wait and then I used to go to the bottom of the lane, and he'd hitch it up, and I used to lead them up.

Mrs Margaret Green

The man with two birthdays

I was born in Reddish in 1915. Like Her Majesty the Queen I have two birthdays. When my father went to register me, he must have given 26 June. He came outside and he was reading this and he realised that a mistake had been made. He went back into the office and said, 'Can you alter this?' which, of course, they can't do. The officer demanded another fee; it was 1915 and the old feller couldn't afford it, could he? So, officially, my birthday is 21 June, and for any business reasons, such as my pension, I've got to abide by 26. Even my call up date for the army was 26. So, actually, the pensions people owe me five days, don't they?

Mr Fred Travis

The violin lesson

I went to learn the violin; my mother brought me a violin from one of the shops or houses where she worked. I went in and the teacher was old. I had to go up a spiral staircase, right to the top floor, then into a little room with a big roaring fire. Through the window I could see the canal down below. I was frightened of the teacher, and when I got home I told my mother I wasn't going again. That were my only violin lesson.

Mrs Lily Gover

Small world, isn't it

I had a carpet cleaner here about twelve months ago. I was asking where he lived and he said 'Hollingworth. I did live in Stalybridge at one time.' 'Whereabouts?' 'At Castle Hall.' 'I was born in Castle Hall.' 'I lived on Kay Street,' he said. 'I was born on Kay Street. What number?' 'I can't remember the number, but it was the top house, below the Rifleman.' I said, 'When I was little, me dad had a shoe shop there, at No. 68.' 'That's the house,' he said, "cos when we moved in there was some lasts and irons down in the cellar. I said to me wife, "There's a shoe-mender's lived here."'

Mr John Perry

To be a boy again

You would play football at night and your fathers would join in. We had many a great game in the bottom of the cemetery or the Butcher's Field, playing football and cricket. It wasn't just the boys, it was the men as well. We used to play Peggy a lot. You had a piece of wood, about four inches long, shaped like a bullet. You would hit it, to get it propelled up into the air, and then give it a whack. The one who hit it furthest was the winner. My wife Barbara's father was a champion at it.

Mr John Perry

Swinging on a lamp-post

We used to like swinging around lamp-posts on a bit of rope that we got from the greengrocer's on King Street. They used to have boxes of oranges and onions delivered, wrapped up with a kind of rope that was like plaited straw. We'd go and beg a piece of this and tie it on a lamp-post and sit in the loop and swing round and round.

Mr Fred Travis

Whit Walks on Kay Street, c. 1912.

Flattening the pins

There were trams, of course, when I was a little girl. There used to be trams coming up Tame Street, which crossed our street. We used to go and put pins on the tram-lines and stand back a bit until a tram passed and flattened them. When we had clog irons on — all the time apart from when we went to church — we used to strike sparks from the tram lines.

Mrs Ethel Anderson

On Shaw Moor

I've never lost the love of Shaw Moor, the moor behind Stalybridge to Mottram. To go over that moor in summer at sunset — you could hear the curlew, and the grouse, the skylark; in summer the cuckoo, up at the Brushes reservoirs. When I was a child, if you were coming over the moors from Mottram on a Sunday afternoon, about six o'clock you would see a forest of mill chimneys, first one, then another, the puff of smoke as they were firing up for Monday morning. Within half an hour they were all puffing away.

Mr Tom Evans

They ruined our canal trip

When we were only about eight or nine we went on this barge. It was just like two planks across you had to sit on. We went on this trip up to Marple. As we were going all these rough lads were rocking the boat. We were

21

terrified when we got off. Wouldn't come back on the barge, so my mother and the friend that were with us had to get tickets to come back on the train.

Miss Annice Ritson

What childhood?

My mother used to wash and sew for folk; so I had to help. When I was only about ten, when I came home from school, I used to have to start doing things. It was a ritual. Monday she used to wash for us; she mangled the clothes. I put them in the mangle and me brother turned the handle. Tuesday I cut a pound and a quarter of shin beef and a quarter of liver for potato pie and beefsteak puddings the day after, then peeled potatoes. Wednesday we used to do the stone floor we had with red ochre; I had to mop the floor Wednesday night. Thursday we used to black-lead in the front room; we used to put all the fire irons on the sofa and cover them up. Friday we just finished off. That were my childhood. She made potato pie Wednesday, beefsteak pudding for Thursday, in a rag, and jam roly-poly for Thursday; Wednesday we always had either pie and custard or pie and rice pudding. Then Friday we always had it in a big dish. Sometimes we had rabbit pie, sometimes we had what we called 'pluck' – it was liver, kidney, all offal. We always had a good dinner.

Mrs May Redford

Just a stroll!

We'd set off for a walk. We'd go up King Street, up Dewsnap Lane, up past what is now Dukinfield Golf Club, up over the top and down to the Rising Moon on Matley Lane. We used to turn left there for the deep cutting, through the deep cutting to Mottram parish church. From there we'd go down into Broadbottom, go up Long Lane, through Charlesworth, up over those rocks there and then reverse and come back home again. It could have easily been twenty miles, y'know.

Mr David Cooper

Holy Trinity Sunday school class, c. 1920. Teacher is Gertie Kenyon.

Whit Walks on Astley Street, Dukinfield, c. 1914. Mr James Cooper is at the front, with a straw hat. The little boy with him is David Cooper.

Giggle-gaggles

When I first went to school, I went to Old St George's – it's a nursing home now. On that corner there are two cottages, Bohemia Cottages, on one side of the steps up to what we call Cocker Hill. At the other corner there used to be a giggle-gaggle and there was a little toffee shop there on that old property. We used to use the giggle-gaggle. Giggle-gaggles are narrow openings; they nearly always go up a slope. They are not very easy to negotiate because they're cobbled. They are very old. There is another giggle-gaggle in Stalybridge, that goes up by Cheetham's Park, where Park Street is. You go to the end of there and that's where the giggle-gaggle is.

Mrs Nellie Howarth

Bluebell Wood

When I was a child, beyond Cheetham Hill Road it was all fields. We kids just roamed the fields and nobody bothered us. You could cut through the golf course and come to Matley Lane and the Rising Moon. We used to go through there to Bluebell Wood, and come out at Bower Fold, Celtic's football ground. We used to go for the day and take a picnic. There were always loads of bluebells growing among the trees. It was like a little wood and a stream ran down it.

Mrs Pat Bolt

The eclipse and the Devil's Chair

That's Hough Hill. Further on there's what we call the Top Wood and the Bottom Wood. They look down on Stalybridge Celtic. 1926

Pat Carthy (Mrs Pat Bolt, left), her cousin, Beryl Grindrod, and Pat's brother, Terence, in the garden of 171 Lodge Lane, in around 1950

I think it was, we all went up, before we went to work – just turned five o'clock in the morning – to the Top Wood with our smoked glasses to watch the eclipse. All the young ones were there; that was more fun than watching the eclipse. There's a road between Top Wood and Bottom Wood that goes right through to Mottram. There's houses all over it now; there were no houses then. There were rocks on the left-hand side, going round the top. We used to play on these rocks and there was one that looked just like a chair. We used to call it the Devil's Chair.

Mrs May Redford

Child Care?

My brother was born with a cleft palate. When he was two, they took him into Pendlebury Hospital. The hospital sorted him out quite well, and in later years he had no speech impediment. But the hospital's idea of child care was that my parents took him in, and then they had to leave him and were not allowed to see him until the day they brought him out. He never saw his mum and dad for a fortnight – the hospital thought that if they visited, he would fret when they left.

Mr Tom Evans

Here comes the *Flying Scotsman*

As kids we used to run up the banking at the back of Victoria Road. The railway was there. One day the *Flying Scotsman* was coming by. It was a very big occasion. We all knew that the *Flying Scotsman* was coming.

Mrs Alice Edwards

Riding the coal lorry

I was five when the General Strike happened. We children took buckets down to the Valley – that was what we called Tame Valley. There were mills down there, all the way to Ashton. We were 'picking'. I was only five and I only knew that I was looking for bits of coke in the piles of ashes from the boiler fires. Later, Mr Pogson used to come round delivering coal with his horse and dray. Mr Pogson's name was Bennett, but they called him Benny. His daughter was my school friend. She used to ride on the back of the dray and pull me up with her when they came to my road. Years later, in the army, I rode in vehicles from two-seaters to three-ton lorries. Nothing ever gave me the buzz that I got from the coal lorry in the twenties.

Mrs Ethel Anderson

'If I catch you...'

One of our enjoyments was standing at the top of Coalpit Hills and looking down on Globe Lane. The Wagon Works was there, and higher up was Kenyon's Rope Works. The Wagon Works was a long, low building, all lit up. Now glass in a window is an invitation to a lad. We used to go up on there and we used to throw stones – well, they did; I never did! They used to throw stones and they used to land them on this building; but they'd gone that far by this time there was no force in them. All at once this chappie would appear, yelling at us, 'If I catch you, I'll...' At that time we were terrified of authority. They only had to say, 'Bobby's coming,' and there were no boys or girls anywhere.

Mr David Cooper

Mr Norman Carthy in the doorway of a shed at Woodmet on Globe Lane, Dukinfield. The Wagon Works is in the background.

2 Family Life

Keeping the family together

I was born in Robinson Street, Stalybridge. We were four children, a brother and three sisters; I was the youngest. My mother died when I was twelve months old, so my dad had to bring us up. Things were rough, but he did his best. He kept us together, and that was something, wasn't it? He could have put us in a home. He worked at Nuttall's at the bottom of Robinson Street; it was a cotton mill, and he was in the spinning room. He had a sister and she took over when she were old enough

Mrs Edith Jones

The hens in the backyard

My mother and auntie weren't working. My mother was on a widow's pension. The house we lived in was near where the Methodist church in Tame Valley is now. I think we had three up and three down, but one was a sort of small box-room and we had a small kitchen; then we had a living room and another room and a cellar. I remember during the war years, if there were a raid on, we'd go down into the cellar. And we had a backyard. I remember, at one stage, when I was younger, we kept some hens in the backyard. We built a little hen-cote to keep them in. They didn't lay very well and we finished up screwing their necks and eating them. That was quite popular when I was younger – people kept hens and after they'd laid the eggs they shared the eggs out.

Mr John Perry

The real hard times

Them days, 1930 up to 1932, was very, very hard. Alice's father didn't know from one week to the next whether he would be working the week after. There was a kind of dole, but it was means tested. If you had anything in the house that would sell and keep you, it had to go. Her father and mine were in the General Strike. Times was very hard.

Mr Les Edwards

Being poor

I'll tell you something about being poor. There were four of us children. For breakfast sometimes, when we had an egg, we had half an egg each. We used to pull our faces if one got a bit more runny yolk than the other. 'He's got a bigger half than me!'

Mrs Alice Edwards

The loving mother, the sympathetic boss and the unfeeling public official.

At the beginning of the war my husband was taken ill with kidney disease. He had one bad do, but he got over that. Then, when it was the Blitz in Manchester and Liverpool, his brother-in-law got wounded. He went down to Liverpool with his sister. It was January, a bad day; he got cold and it started his kidneys again; he died in the August 1941, just before our Philip was three. I was working because we needed the money. My mother looked after Philip. We'd never have got through if it hadn't 'a been for my mother. She was an angel. I had to go to work while my husband was poorly, and my mother used to come down and see to him. I had a good boss. He let me come home at lunch time to see him, then I'd come home again at dinner-time, and then I'd come home again at three to see he were all right. Not many bosses would have let me do that. I used to get 10s a week for me and 5s a week for Philip. When you're a widow they tax your widow's pension and they were taking more off me than they were giving me. I went to the tax office to see if they could do anything about it. When I told him the case – that Philip were poorly and he had to have a lot of nourishment – he said, 'That's your worry, not ours.' That was how they treated you in them days.

Mrs May Redford

Workhouse girl

When my mother was only a girl she had her foot off. Because she was illegitimate, she was brought up in the workhouse. She told me a rhyme that they had to say every morning before their breakfast. 'Harriet is my name, a pauper is my station; and Christ is my salvation.' When they grew up they were already marked; they were traumatized anyhow, weren't they. For somebody like my father, who was brought up strictly a Primitive Methodist, all bright and shiny – he was a local preacher at seventeen – to marry such a girl! But marry they did, a decision not well received by the family. So we were left largely on our own.

Mr David Cooper

A mother's lot

There were five of us children. The oldest girl was called Amy; then I came next, Alex; then Edith; then there was William; then there was Alice; finally there was John. My mother was left with five of us after my dad died. She had to go to work. She was a weaver before she married my dad, so she had to go back. She'd been out of it that long, it was very difficult. People was very good. All the neighbours round about they had a collection for her. She went into Harrison's mill as a weaver. She had a very hard time. She used to come home sometimes and just lie on the settee and she'd be there until bedtime.

Mr Alex Cox

Good people

My mother was more strict than my father was, but I think she had more of the worry of it. Mother used to talk to us more sharply than my dad did. If you wanted to do anything, my dad would say, 'You'd better ask your mother.' My mother'd say, 'See what your dad says.' So we'd go back to my dad – 'If it's all right with your mother, it's all right with me,' he'd say. We had a big rocking chair. It didn't matter who was in it; when my mother walked in, we always stood up. My dad always referred to her as 'mother' – 'See what mother says' – which was nice. When my dad was working he used to wear laced-up boots. We'd go and undo his laces for him. When we were all grown up, my mother adopted a boy. His father died in January 1940, when he was just two years old. My mother looked after him quite a lot. His mother was in hospital away much of the time. When he was five, she died. My mother and father adopted him legally and he called them mummy and daddy High. They were good people to do that.

Mrs Alice Edwards

Getting out of Castle Hall

I felt sorry for my mother. She didn't want a big family. Having been the eldest of eight, she'd been with her mother when she had miscarriages as well as the children. She'd always had to stop off work when the baby arrived. After she was married, she didn't have me for five years and they really wanted a boy. Then she thinks, 'I can make these pretty dresses,' and I, a tomboy, wouldn't wear them. As a girl she lived up Castle Hall and she couldn't leave quickly enough, 'cos in those days it was rough, with fighting an'all. As a girl she had to go out and clean toilets, six toilets at a penny each. She didn't get one penny; it all went into the family purse. So she couldn't wait to get away. When she married my dad, they got this lovely house to rent, down North End, near the canal. She got it just how she wanted it. Then my dad came out of work. So they had to look for somewhere else. These houses up Castle Hall were owned by the Birches, which my mother was before she married. So the moved back to Castle Hall, to the house at Kay Street, which was the house she'd left to get married.

Mrs Jean Pilling

Elizabeth Anne Birch, whose family owned houses on Kay Street, where Jean Travis's (Mrs Jean Pilling's) mother lived as a girl and as a married woman.

My mother and father

My mother was the strictest. You had to be in for a certain time; whatever time you told her, you had to be there. If there was any chastising, my mother did it. She would often say, 'I'll tell your father,' but that didn't bother us. We used to look forward to father coming home from work. We always had a big fire, of course, with father working at the colliery. We used to sit round and father was a great one for telling stories, and he loved poetry; so of course, we all had to have this poetry in us turns. He'd have us all singing. He'd make toys; he was always making little toys out of bits of wood and matchboxes and things. We hadn't much money, but we were never short of anything, as far as toys he could make for us. Mother was the one that kept us in order. It was, 'Sit on that chair and don't move,' or 'Don't swing your legs,' or 'That's it. I've had enough. Go upstairs.' We were more frightened of my mother than my father.

Miss Annice Ritson

Sunday visiting

After chapel on Sunday my mother used to come straight home to get the dinner ready. My dad used to take me to where we used to

Ritson family group at the back of 121 Railway Street, Dukinfield.

live in Zetland Street. My uncle – he wasn't really my uncle, but we'd lived next door to him in Zetland Street – used to brew Dandelion and Burdock, and I loved Dandelion and Burdock. From there we used to go on Combermere Street, to an auntie of mine, and then on to Brunswick Street. There was a shop there, a little mixed business; we used to have a look round there and then we'd come home for dinner. My father used to buy me a drink there in that shop, which was lovely. The shop was called Williams'.

Mr Kenneth Gee

Knowl Street in the 1930s

I was born in Knowl Street, which is off Portland Place, at the very bottom of Mottram Road. There were six little houses. The family in the first house were called Edwards; they had six children. Next door were the Goddards, who were elderly; I don't think they had any children. In the next house was my grandmother Eastwood. In the next one were the Braddocks, who went to live in Mottram. Then came us, the Kay family. Next door to us were the Shaws, who had two young children. The house we lived in was a two-up, two-down. There was no back door;

Williams' mixed business on Brunswick Street, Dukinfield.

row, my mum's sister, her husband and her daughter lived. Then my mum's eldest sister, her husband and three children lived at the other end of the row. My mum came from Stalybridge, but my dad was from Dukinfield.

Mrs Pat Bolt

Getting the dinner

My dad didn't like me mum's mother, nor she him. He didn't like my mother doing a lot for her mother, so I used to go grandma's errands for her. During the war, when rationing was on, we used to go to – I can't remember what it was called, but it's still there, across the way from the Catholic church in Dukinfield – it was like a restaurant. Grandma used to have little pots and basins; she used to send me down and you could get a dinner there, and I used to have my dinner with her. I can remember getting hotpot, and potato pies and things with crusts on. It was only a couple of pence.

Mrs Vera Win Hotchkiss

the house came to the edge of the river. When you came out of the house there was dirt. Then, at the end there were three toilets, one toilet for two families. That doesn't sound very good, but they were spotless; they whitewashed them clean. There was also a midden. That's where all the dust, ashes and tin cans were put. We didn't have dustbins. We took everything to the midden.

Mrs Joyce Hall

Staying close

I was born on Frederick Street, Denton. We came to live on Lodge Lane, Dukinfield. We lived on the left-hand side. On the right-hand side, in the end house, my grandma and grandad Thomas lived. In the middle of the

Mortality rate

We weren't a large family. Though there tended to be large families at the start of the twentieth century, there also tended to be early deaths. Altogether there were eight children born to my parents, but only five survived. The other three died; one was a couple of days old; another was a month old.

Mr David Cooper

My friend Alice

My grandmother died in 1914, when I were nine. My father took me upstairs and she were in the coffin. It were the first time I'd seen a dead person. He had to lift me up to show me.

Wedding of Tom Birch and Kitty. Lily Birch is the bridesmaid.

Didn't bother me. All that bothered me, she had a penny in both eyes. All I said was. 'Eh, she's got two pennies.' It didn't bother me. There was a little girl lived two doors from me at one time; she was my age. She lived at 32 Cheetham Hill Road, next door to grandpa at 30. I used to call her mum 'auntie' and she did the same with mine. We were always in each other's houses. It was not long before Christmas. Her mother and father had got up. They had a fire in her bedroom, but it had no screen around it. Alice, my friend, were in bed, and her father said, 'Don't get out of bed. Stop in bed. We're going to bring you a drink up.' Well, Alice got out of bed. They had a little mantle-piece; only a small fireplace. Her nightdress got on fire and it burned her; it killed her. I remember going in and seeing her when she were in her coffin. My mother had bought a bunch of flowers. I took 'em and her mother said, 'Do you want to see Alice?' I said, 'Yes.' I looked at her; can see her now. She had a little silver brooch pinned on, said 'Alice,' and some lilies of the valley in it, and

31

her hair – she were blonde – it were just trimmed. I went home, and I said to my mother, 'She's not dead. She's just asleep.' She looked proper nice.

Miss Lily Birch

Back Vaudrey Street

I was born in Back Vaudrey Street, Stalybridge in 1930. Our house was a two-up and two-down. It had an outside toilet at the far end of the garden at the back. You had a little route march down to the toilet. Then y'had to make sure there were no-one in before you, because families had to share the toilet. It wasn't just for you. My uncle Walter and auntie Alice also lived in the street. Mr Barraclough lived next door to us; he were my auntie's father, y'see, and he were on his own. Then there were the Hydes. Then uncle Bob and my grandma Sleigh lived in the next one. Then there were the Dearnleys at the top. There was a man and wife in between; they were in the Salvation Army – can't think of their names. Then, on the other side was Gillebrands, and auntie Alice and uncle Walter. In the next house they were called Spence, or something like that.

Mr Bob Sleigh

My auntie in Bohemia Cottages

One of my mother's sisters, my auntie Edith, lived in one of those Bohemia Cottages. They are in Portland Place and are very old, 170-something. Two little cottages near some steps that led to what was Old St George's (or was it New St George's?) on Wakefield Road. She lived in this little cottage where she was married, my auntie Edith, and she had her only child there. I remember walking with the scholars one particular Whit Friday. It was absolutely pouring down, and they put the banners over us to keep us dry. My auntie must have seen me and I remember her running down to give me an umbrella, and a raincoat to put on to keep me dry until we got back to church.

Mrs Joyce Travis

Stoning the steps

We used to stone the step and the portion of the pavement in front. You mopped it, then you stoned it with this stuff, which was soft, like sandstone. Your window ledge might be stoned as well, and the back step and the toilet. Donkey stone came in three colours – white, cream and yellow. The colour came off the donkey stone. Some people used to do patterns. I hated the yellow; to me it was a really horrible yellow. I wasn't too keen on the white; my auntie always used white. We used cream. Friday morning all the mothers are out there. My dad used to say, 'Clean things on; clean steps; that's when the money comes home.'

Mrs Ethel Anderson

Polishing the brasses

In those days they had open fires. Everything went on the fire in them days; there was no such thing as dustbins – everything was burned on the fire. We had a big open fireplace. We had a steel fender, a posh one it was; a pair of steel tongs, with brass knobs on, a steel poker with a brass head on, and a steel shaft with a brass head on with a little shovel at the bottom. They all had to be cleaned every week. They had to shine like silver – and they were never used. They were just ornamental.

Mr Alex Cox

Bohemia Cottages.

The lady with the hoover

The house would usually be cleaned with a brush and shovel. Every now and again, a lady who lived on Tower Street – she always seemed to me a little bit posher than us, but she was a nice lady – was kind enough to lend my mother this hoover. She was the one lady I remember who had a hoover. Then our house would get a really good clean. The hoover used to frighten me. When it started up, I'd run out of the house. It was just something that was alien to me.

Mr John Perry

A glass of sarsaparilla

When we were young and all the mills finished work, we used to go to meet our aunties down King Street. All you could hear was the patter of clogs along Tame Valley and up King Street. We used to go to the herbalist's, Hurst's on King Street, and have drinks. They used to sell sarsaparilla. We used to meet our aunties and they used to say, 'Suppose you want some sarsaparilla?' We used to go to the herbalist's and have a glass of sarsaparilla.

Miss Annice Ritson
and Mrs Leslie Preston

33

Mr and Mrs Alfred Travis, on their son Fred's motorcycle.

How to buy an engagement ring

In May 1941 I'd been out in the Middle East a short time when I got a letter from home – 'The police have been round. They want you to take the contact breaker out of your motorcycle and hide it.' That was when there was a threat of paratroopers being dropped; they thought they might get the motorcycle and use it, y'see. I instructed a friend of mine, George Booth, to do what the police wanted. Months afterwards another letter – 'The police have been round again. They want you to take the engine out and bury it.' I told my friend to sell it. It was a 490 Norton. He sold it for me for £30. I used the £30 to buy an engagement ring for Joyce.

Mr Fred Travis

Being poor

My father was a clerk. Because he was often ill he had to get any jobs that were going. He was never able to keep one for long. If you were ill, you were ill and you were off work. There was no sick pay or anything like that. The only relief was the Poor Law relief. When I hear people nowadays talk about being poor, they don't know what poor is. One day a fellow who lived in Fitzroy Street saw my dad. He said, 'There's a job coming up in the Poor Law offices. Put in an application.' He did and he got the job – Assistant Poor Relieving Officer for Dukinfield. He wasn't particularly keen about it. He had to go in people's houses and assess what they had, and whether they sold ornaments and things – that was how the law looked at things in those days.

Mr David Cooper

'Jerry' for short

Many people will remember the days when the doctor's man came round on a Friday night collecting the 3d or 6d. That was a common thing in this area. The doctor was Dr William Chambers Thomas. His wife, Enid

Thomas, was also a doctor and she used to call him Jerry. He came from Beaumaris. I was the first baby he delivered in Stalybridge.

Mr Tom Evans

Saturday night outing

When we lived on Zetland Street – I left there when I were five – on Saturday night we used to walk down to Ashton market. They were selling food cheap then, which they couldn't keep. Every Saturday night that was our outing, to walk from Zetland Street down Crescent Road to Ashton market to get this stuff and bring it back home.

Mr Kenneth Gee

My family in Millbrook

I were born in 4 Brick Houses, Millbrook, in April, 1905. There were nine of us children and my mother and father. My mother always used to say about me, 'She's a cheeky little madam, that one!' I was the youngest girl, and the middle one of the nine. There was Elizabeth, Annie, Maggie, William, Alice (that's me!), Matthew, Joe, Edward and George. When I were three we went a'living in Stamford Street. I said, 'I'm stopping here.' My mother said, 'Well, stop on your own.'

Mrs Alice Young

The Yorkshireman and the politician

My dad was a forthright Yorkshireman, born in Dewsbury. He was a good father and a good husband. My mother was taken away from school at eleven to look after the family. She was very ill-educated academically, but she could do anything. Up to starting work I never had a bought garment. She made them

all. She had a hard life. She was also a forthright politician.

Mr James Wainwright

On a tricycle to Castle Hall

My grandfather had a baker's shop. It was my uncle who was the baker; he served his time. My grandfather used to go all the way from the Hague, all the way into town and all the way up again to Castle Hall on this three wheeler. I suppose he had regular customers up there. He also used to serve the Drill Hall up there; when they had any functions on he would provide the cakes and whatnot. He worked very hard, because he did all the oven work as well. He was only about six stone, wet through. He was very quiet. My grandma would make a fool of him in the shop and he'd just trot off about his business.

Mrs Joyce Travis

'Where've you been?'

When I first met Alice I used to bike it up here practically every day, all the way from Eccles to Railway Street, Dukinfield. We would go to the pictures and we used to ask her father for permission to go to the first house. If we were late, he was stood at the front door. There was an entry down Lime Street; we'd be stood there kissing goodnight, and he'd come and look for us. 'Where've you been,' he'd say.

Mr Les Edwards

Courting a Tame Valley girl

When I was courting Betty, I would walk down Tame Valley to see her. I was a stranger there, so my appearance in the valley caused some comment and curtain twitching. Once,

Kenneth Gee, aged two, on Lime Street. He used to go on a Saturday night outing to Ashton with his mother.

Joyce Hassall's (Mrs Joyce Travis') grandad and grandma Hassall, who had the baker's shop.

as I was walking along the valley, I met a fellow. He said, 'I hear you're coming to join us in the valley.' 'I am,' I answered. 'Ever had pneumonia?' he asked. 'No,' I replied. 'Well you bloody soon will have, coming to live down here.'

Mr David Jones

Showing off your Whitsun clothes

At Whitsuntide, because I was the eldest in our family, I had to take my cousin Frank and his sister round to show our Whitsun clothes. We went up to the top of Castle Hall, just before the Drill Hall. We had a lot of family lived up there. Every house you entered, 'Come on, let's have a look!' Your clothes went up, and they had a look at your knickers. We came out; it was usually a 3d bit from family, 1d from most other places. You used to have gangs of kids, all over the town, from different parts of the town, going off to show their new clothes. The boys had to open their jackets to show their shirts.

Mrs Ethel Anderson

A family home on Tame Valley in the 1920s

We had a six-roomed house. My mum and dad lived with mi grandma and grandad. My grandad Senior, my mother's father, was a tailor. He used to work from his home. When grandad and grandma died, mum and dad had the house. It was all right for a family of seven, mum and dad and five of us children. We'd no cooker; food was cooked on an old-fashioned fireplace. Mum did all her cooking on that. She used to have to black-lead it, and she kept it lovely. There was an old slop-stone. No hot water, only cold. By the side of the fireplace

Mr and Mrs Willie Taylor, c. 1912. James is on his dad's lap, Nellie on her mother's.

Where's the ginnel?

I lived at 48 Park Road as a child. You were all poor then. There were very few people who seemed well off. You were all in the same boat. Everybody was friendly. You were all in it together. You were all equal. You could go in anyone's house. They called the street I lived on the New Row; it was the longest row in Dukinfield without a ginnel. It should have had a ginnel halfway up. Florrie Ash used to say that her house should have been the ginnel. It might as well have been left as a ginnel, because everybody just walked through, instead of going right round the long road. You didn't lock your door. They either used to go in the front door or the back door and shout, 'It's only me', and pass through. It was friendly; it was a happy time!

Mrs Barbara Perry

was like a boiler. Dad used to fill that when we had to have a bath in front of the fire, the old-fashioned zinc bath. He used to put water in it to get warm from the fire and then we used to have to tip it in the bath. We didn't have electricity, only gas mantles. When my brother James was studying to be a local preacher, we'd no gas in the back room that he shared with my brother Frederick. So they had to have a candle. There was a gas mantle in my room and in mum and dad's room, but not in theirs. There was a garden at the back that came onto Chadwick's mill; there was no garden at the front. There was an outside toilet. We had a front room, living room, kitchen and three bedrooms. Outside the front door the trams used to come by; we had trams passing all the time. We used to have the pitter-patter of clogs passing the window, going to the mills.

Mrs Betty Jones

'Our Jeck'

My grandparents had a butcher's shop on Market Street, near the town hall. The front room upstairs was absolutely enormous. My auntie Annie had her wedding reception in that great big sitting room. It was always called the sitting room. My grandparents had a dog, a short-haired terrier called Jack. My grandma used to say, 'Our Jeck.' At a party there this man was sat at t the top of a winding staircase with a full trifle. He was a bit inebriated and it must have all got a bit much for him. He put the trifle on the floor and went somewhere. The next thing I remember was my grandma coming along. 'Eh, look at this! Our Jeck's eaten the whole trifle.' The dog had had a whale of a time.

Mrs Joyce Travis

Slum houses and magic

Joyce Hassall's (Mrs Joyce Travis') grandad and grandma Drury in the doorway of their butcher's shop on Market Street, Stalybridge.

Dukinfield Hall

Down at the bottom of Astley Street, where Globe Square is, that were Dukinfield Hall. I used to go through Dukinfield Hall going to work. There were houses on either side of the railings. My sister-in-law, Mary, was born in Dukinfield Hall and lived down there. There was the Tudor Accumulator Works on one side; they were very busy. Men used to be coming up from Guide Bridge – they must have got off a train there – to work at the Accumulator Works and the Wagon Works. I used to pass them. There were rows of streets. It was quite a little village down there and quite a lot of people lived there.

Mrs Nellie Preston

The houses on Knowl Street, where I lived as a child, were demolished. One day they came to tell us that they were condemned under the slum clearance regulations. It went down very, very hard. My mother was so terribly upset; our house were poor, but it were spotless. They explained that we would be re-housed on this new estate that was being built on the outskirts of Stalybridge, near the moorland Everybody would be re-housed in beautiful homes. The deadline came, and this was the terrible part. Everything had to be put into boxes, ready for eight o'clock the morning you were moving. A lorry came, pulled by horses, a big lorry, closed up. Everything went into that lorry, your clothes, your furniture, everything. When that lorry left your house, you had to leave with it. They put wood to barricade you out; you were not allowed back in. That lorry went to Stalybridge market ground and they put fumigating stuff inside the lorry and it was all sealed up. It was all fumigated, on chance you had fleas or bugs. It was a showing up, but everybody had to have it done. That left the only thing that wasn't fumigated – us with the clothes that we were wearing. You were not allowed into your new house, you couldn't even have the key, until you'd been fumigated. We went to some place – I can only remember that it was up High Street – and we went into this room and some men said, 'Go in there; take all your clothes off and put them in this drum. When you've put everything in this drum, your clothes, your shoes, turn the drum round.' Then there was a big bath filled with hot water, and soap. I had only ever had a bath in a tin bath. I thought it was wonderful. We got in this lovely warm bath. My mum was sitting on a little seat, crying; she was feeling the shame. When we'd had this bath, we had to knock and the drum came back, and our clothes were all warm and lovely. We had to go and sign and we could have the key to the new house. When we went into the new house, it was empty; the furniture hadn't arrived. When it did arrive, it smelled of all this horrible fumigating stuff. We had to have the windows open and it was bitter cold. But, to me, it was like moving into Buckingham Palace. Press a switch and a light came on; we had a bathroom, where you could have a bath with hot water. We had a front garden and a back garden. And we had a toilet in the house! Also, from living in a little backwater, with no view, we had the wonderful view of the moors. I heard the skylark, and I heard the cuckoo, which I'd never heard before in my life. I was ten years old. It was magic,

Mrs Joyce Hall

Uncle George's chippy

As a child I knew that I was being well looked-after. I had a great love for my mother and my auntie. The man next door, George Crossland, had a chip-shop. I always knew him as Uncle George, though he wasn't really my uncle. I used to come home every dinnertime from school, have my dinner and then walk back for the afternoon session. Mainly we came through the cemetery, because there was a sort of path through the cemetery. Then, on the way back my uncle George would call me into the chip shop and I'd be walking up the road, back to school, with a bag of chips. I were always well-fed.

Mr John Perry

Picnic in Matley Woods

My mother told us that they used to have a market at the back of Dukinfield Town Hall, and they used to have Dukinfield Wakes, and a fairground on Chapel Street. I remember Matley Woods. Mother and father used to take us up there on picnics on a Sunday.

Miss Annice Ritson

Picnic in Matley Woods. Joyce, Nellie and Harry Ritson with their mother, Eva.

Mr and Mrs Harry Anderson's wedding. They are on the steps of Booth Street Methodist church, Stalybridge.

The house on New Bridge Street

Before the war we moved from Castle Hall to what they called New Bridge Street. It was right at the side of the canal. It had big bedrooms and in one bedroom we even had a toilet. We had a toilet downstairs so we had two in the house. We had hot water and electricity and a little bathroom. It actually had a shower in it. There was a big cellar that had a big stone slab, a sink, a set-pot boiler and a fireplace. In the air raids we used to go down there. The family next door used to come with us. In another part of this cellar was the coal place. In the back part, which came underneath the kitchen, Ben Woodall had his wood for making coffins. You could always tell when he was busy, because in th' middle of the night you could hear him sorting his wood out. Also we could see them fishing. Men used to come on th'canal; they'd sit there all day.

Mr Bob Sleigh
and Mrs Lily Gover

My Methodist family

My brothers were James and Joseph; my sister was Florence. I was the fourth child. I used to go to dinner every Sunday to my auntie's parents' home. Their son, my auntie's brother, used to carry me to Booth Street Methodist church when I was two years old. My parents went to Booth Street. I've been a Methodist all my life. When my husband died last year, it was so sudden, I didn't know whether I was coming or going. The love from people at my church – Stalybridge Methodist – was almost tangible.

Mrs Ethel Anderson

41

3 Schooldays

Crescent Road school, 1914-18

Mixed infants and slate pencils

I went to Crescent Road council school – the Board school, we called it. Over the doorway it said, 'Mixed Infants.' I was one of the Mixed Infants. I remember we were issued with slates with wooden frames and a piece of rag, and you'd a tin can with some water so you could rub out what you'd written. We wrote with slate pencils, the squeakier the better; the girls all said, 'Oooh!' and the boys did it again. At seven I went to the big school. The school was girls underneath and boys on the top. There were a wall between us. We'd nothing to do with girls. Didn't know girls existed. Can't remember the name of the head teacher. The first class teacher I had upstairs was Miss Sally Rogers.

Mr David Cooper

The great explosion

I was in Standard 1 at the time of the explosion in Dukinfield – well, it was in Ashton, but the effects were felt all round. We were in

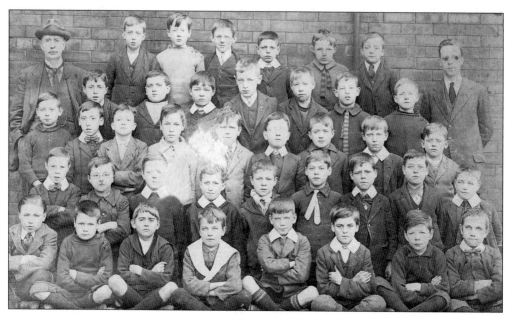

Crescent Road school, c. 1921. Back row, left: George Robert Marshall (headmaster); right, Mr Cowling.

Crescent Road school, 1917, Standard 1. The teacher (back row, left) is Miss Sally Rogers.

school that afternoon; a hot, sunny day it was. All at once there was this huge bang. The headmaster – he was called 'Snotty Bob'; he was a magistrate and the rumour was that he could put you in prison if you didn't behave yourself – was at the top of the stairs trying to stop the children from running. He hadn't a ghost of a chance; they were between his legs, under his arms, everywhere; he was lucky he didn't get knocked down. We were down those stone steps in a minute, not that we knew what to do when we got outside, but we had to get out. There was this horrible smell; I can smell it now. TNT explosion they called it; there were a lot of people killed.

Mr David Cooper

The catch flew off the window

Our classroom had windows that were the kind where you pull a catch and the window opens inward. When the explosion took place in Ashton, the catch flew off one of the windows and it hit our teacher, Sally Rogers, on the nose. Were you sorry for Sally, who had a stick and knew just how to use it, and used it if she needed to, or were you tough like lads are?

Mr David Cooper

The long walk to school

I started school in 1927. I went to Crescent Road School. Had to go all round the river and up Crescent Road. Later I had to go to the Moravian school. Went up Old Hall Road, then up to the Moravian church and the school was on the right. When I was eleven I went on to Lakes Road girls' school. That was just off Pickford Lane, so I had all that long way to walk. You walked along Tame Valley, up Tower Street and it brought you to Pantomime Brew steps; you come up by the cemetery, and then along Foundry

Moravian Junior school, 1931, Form 3. Second row, far right, Betty Taylor (Mrs Betty Jones).

Street; then onto Pickford Lane and through to school. It was quite a long walk. We had to come home for our dinner, then back again, all the same way. I can't remember much about the teachers. I remember that while I was at Crescent Road, this boy threw a pen at the teacher; it misfired and caught her hair. I don't remember anything about the Moravian school. I was happy at Lakes Road; I liked netball, I was a games leader and I used to play hockey. The headmistress was Mrs Wood. She was a very nice lady. Miss Lodge, the music teacher, lived on Stockport Road in Ashton.

Mrs Betty Jones

Crescent Road Infants' School, 1920s

I went to school in Gorton for about twelve months when I was three years old. Then we moved to my father's mother in Ashton. She had a cycle store on Oldham Road and we lived there for a little while. I went to Gatefield school. Then my parents decided to move back to my grandmother Bickerdyke's and I went to Crescent Road school. We were there in the infants, then we moved to the juniors; then, when we were eleven years old, they divided us – the boys stayed at Crescent Road and the girls went to the Moravian school. I went to the Moravian until Lakes

Road school was built. I was in the second year of the seniors then and we all moved to Lakes Road. At Crescent Road we used slates for writing, with a slate pencil. We always used to play in a separate schoolyard. They kept the younger ones together and you didn't mix with the older ones until you were a little bit older. We had the frames, y'know, the abacus frames with the beads on, for counting. I remember when we were juniors they had a French teacher at Crescent Road. 'Course, when we went to Lakes Road, we had a French mistress, and the school had netball pitches, a hockey pitch, tennis courts and each class had their own little garden that they had to do.

Miss Annice Ritson

A warm drink at playtime

I didn't like school very much. There wasn't any special reason; I think I just liked to be at home with my mother. We had some lovely teachers. I can remember my mother, when it were cold weather, bringing us a warm drink at playtime. She'd come and push it through the railings.

Mrs Nellie Preston

Horlicks

When we were in the juniors at Crescent Road, you used to pay I think it were threepence a week and you had a glass of Horlicks at the playtime. There was this little room and you used to go in and they used to give us a glass of Horlicks.

Miss Annice Ritson

Crescent Road council school, c. 1925. Teacher is Mrs Kellet.

Staff of Moravian school (Date unknown).

'But mum, I'll be late again!'

They had the cane at Crescent Road. If you were late, which I often was, you got the cane. Being the eldest, I used to have to go errands before I went to school. The shops didn't open until nine o'clock. I always knew I was going to be late. The children all used to assemble in the big hall first; they played hymns and said prayers. If you were late, you walked at the side and sat down along the sides. After the assembly was over, you all had to queue up and have the cane for being late – girls as well. I used to tell my mother, 'I'm going to be late.' She used to say, 'It doesn't make any difference,' and I had to do the errand first. I used to pelt up to school, hoping to get in first, but I knew I couldn't. They caned us on our hands; just used to lick it afterwards.

Miss Annice Ritson

Counting with sea-shells

I went to Crescent Road council school. When I was a bit older I went to the Moravian school; the boys stopped at Crescent Road and the girls moved to the Moravian school. It was on Old Road in Dukinfield. The Moravian church was there, but it's been pulled down now. When I started school I remember using a slate and chalk, and I can remember counting with sea-shells, little sea-shells.

Mrs Evelyn Whitworth

Lead Us, Heavenly Father, Lead Us, to the baths

I went to Crescent Road school in the 1930s. One time we were having assembly. We used to sing a hymn and we had a prayer. Our class weren't singing properly. Our teacher was Mr Kimberley. First thing after assembly we used to go to the baths. We used to have to walk from Dukinfield, down Crescent Road, down King Street, round Wharf Street across the canal to Ashton baths. That took probably a half-hour; then you had half an hour in the baths; then you walked back again. Well, you always had Oxo after the baths, which tasted good. This particular morning assembly was over. We went in the classroom to get us towels and trunks, all ready for going to the baths. Mr Kimberley says, 'Right. Sit down. You weren't singing that hymn. You're going to learn every word before you go to the baths.' And we had to learn every word of 'Lead Us, Heavenly Father, Lead Us' off by heart before he would let us go.

Mr Kenneth Gee

Crescent Road school, 1940s

Cocoa powder and a nap

I started at Crescent Road Infants school, then the Moravian school, then Lakes Road Girls'. I can remember going to school in 1944,

when I started, walking in the snow. I used to take a tin of some description. They used to fill it with cocoa powder at school and then you used to bring it home. There was hardly any of it left because you used to spend all day dipping your finger in it. I suppose the cocoa powder must have had vitamins in it, or something. When I first went to school, in the afternoon they used to put all these mats on the floor and y'had to lie down and have a sleep.

Mrs Barbara Perry

A far from ideal football pitch

I enjoyed my schooldays mainly because of the sport. I was always into sport – cricket and football. I remember that, when I was at Crescent Road boys' school, we didn't have a football pitch close at hand. When it came to the football period, we used to have to walk up to a pitch, which was near Lakes Road school. It used to have a great rut running across the goal area. No matter how often you filled it in, it would start to sink again. I remember scoring a goal; I hit the ball along the ground, it hit this rut; the goalkeeper dived and it went over his head. Football pitches weren't quite like they are today!

Mr John Perry

Wesleyan school, Stalybridge, 1914-15

And all because of my sister!

My oldest sister was Amy. I had another sister called Alice. That one was a terror, always complaining, she wasn't doing this and she wasn't doing that. One day the older sister came to me and said, 'Alex, our Alice is not going to school.' 'How d'you mean? I saw her go in the yard.' 'Yes,' she said, 'but she's gone into the cloakroom as if she were hanging her clothes up, then, when everyone's gone upstairs, she's put them on again and come out.' I had to give her a good talking to. It meant that I couldn't go to Wesleyan till I'd made sure she'd gone in and stopped in. That used to make me late. Mr Harmer, the Wesleyan headmaster, were a devil for being punctual. Soon as it were nine o'clock he'd blow his whistle and everybody were in. Then he'd come to yard gate, down at the bottom of Canal Street, and he had his cane in his hand. He'd be blowing his whistle for to make latecomers hurry up. Nearly every morning I were a few minutes late. Very, very rarely could I get in on time. He'd wait outside the door, and as you skipped in, he'd whack the back of your legs with the cane. He were a terror for it. Mr Harmer had a daughter called Florence. She were teaching at Wesleyan and eventually she took her mother's place when she retired. They were two terrors, mother and father, in day school, but in Sunday school they were beautiful. You couldn't fault them.

Mr Alex Cox

Lily and Miss Redison's cushion

I went to Wesleyan school, down Canal Street. There was an engineering works, Wainwright's, and then the school was on the side. I went there until I was fourteen. Miss Harmer was head teacher. Miss Redison was one of the teachers in the primary. I used to like a cup of Oxo at the break time, playtime like. The school gave us that, probably about 1d. When we was in the primary with Miss Redison we had the little slate boards to chalk on. Miss Redison was very good, because she always had a cushion. If you was tired, she'd let you go to sleep. She'd give you the cushion to put on the table where you were sat, and you could put your head down and go to sleep. I

loved that teacher; I thought she was smashing!

Mrs Lily Gover

St John's school, Dukinfield

The early 1920s

I went to St John's school. It was a nice school, a good school. The headmaster was Mr Taylor. There was a Mr Radcliffe and my teacher was Miss Keighley. Then, when you got to eleven, you had to go to Central school in Stalybridge. At St John's in the first class, Miss Thornley's, we used slates and wrote on them with a slate pencil. Our Harry used to take me to school every morning, up that brew. Across the way from St John's there was a little toffee shop. In them days a halfpenny were a lot to you. When my dad was going out to work, he used to give me and my sister – who were only twelve month older than me – a penny between us. We used to go for haporth of toffee. My sister was called Martha. At St John's we used to go into church on Ash Wednesday, and they used to put ashes on our heads.

Mrs Edith Jones

St John's schoolteachers, 1920s

I went to St John's school; the headmaster was Mr Taylor. The headmistress, over the tinies, was Miss Crook, a Queen Victoria-style lady. A few of the teachers are still living. The first teacher was Miss Wainwright; the second one was Mrs Roe, who was in my mother's class at school. My mother was chosen, with two other scholars, to go to be trained as a teacher, but her mother died and she had to leave school because she was the eldest. The school board gave her an engraved workbox and a guinea, a golden guinea, because it was such a disappointment to her. Then there was Mrs

St John's school, 1929, Class 3.

Booth, a wonderful teacher and a real martinet. Then came Miss Blocksage, who is still going strong. There was a lady who went to be a missionary; she was a good teacher, but a very strict, irascible lady. Then there was Miss Keighley, Bertha Keighley. Mr Gilbert came; he was only very young and, when he left, Mr Ashburner came. We wrote on slates with a slate pencil. We did have chalk for some things, but I don't know what. The pencil was a piece of slate shaped like a pencil. You couldn't rub things out. I can see her now, Miss Wainwright, in the first class, coming round with a piece of rag like a dish mop and a bowl. She'd wet the rag and then you'd have to wet the slate and rub it then to clean it off.

Mrs Ethel Anderson

St John's in the late 1930s

I went to school in 1937. The headmaster was Mr Radcliffe. He was also a sidesman/warden of the church. We always had Religious Studies every morning. You daren't be late for school because that was the first thing on the agenda. He waited for you and, if you hadn't been to church on Sunday, you knew about it. The first thing I can remember about going to school is that we used to write in sand. We didn't have paper; we had trays of sand. You used your finger; you used to have to form letters in the sand, then scrub them and do it again. The first few years of my school life they had beautiful people there. Miss Booth was red-haired and she always wore one of those big cartwheel-hearing things; she lived

49

down the bottom of Cheetham Hill Road. Mrs Duckworth was the very first teacher I had. Then you went into – but I can't remember her name. My sister got caned on the hand for not spelling CAT. Miss Booth did that.

Mrs Vera Win Hotchkiss

Grandma and the headmaster

At St John's, when you went in the main door, there was a stairs going up – green marble, green, glittery marble. I was in assembly and the headmaster shouted me out; he said I'd been talking. I said I hadn't. 'You're answering

Mrs Eliza (Lizzie) Harrop, maternal grandmother of Vera Win Owens (Mrs Vera Win Hotchkiss).

me back,' he said. 'I'm not; I'm telling you the truth.' He dragged me to his study at the top of the stairs. His cane was thick; it was a rod and a half. 'Hand out. If you weren't talking, you answered me back.' I was screaming, more with temper than anything. When I got home my grandmother was in the house. She took one look at my hand; it was swollen by this time. Johnny Bant's was at the back of the house and you walked through the fields to St John's. My grandmother gets me back to school. We gets in through the door and she spots him at the top of the stairs. 'You! Come down here.' She played hell with him because of the state of my hand. It was always my grandmother who stood up for me.

Mrs Vera Win Hotchkiss

St John's in the early 1940s

I started at St John's in 1942, when I was five. We had the church attached and on Ash Wednesday we always went into the church. Next door was a hall, and that was where we had our pantomimes when we went to Sunday school. Miss Blocksage, Miss Booth and Miss Adshead were at St John's. There was one who taught us to knit, on steel needles with cotton thread. Miss Blocksage had a ruler; y'had to behave or she'd clock you with it. I liked school. We used to walk to St John's across the fields. In 1947 there was deep snow and we had to walk across the railings. I didn't stop off school; if you didn't go to school, they wouldn't let you be in the pantomime.

Mrs Pat Bolt

Hob Hill school, Stalybridge, c. 1910

I went to Hob Hill school in Stalybridge. The headmistress was Miss Roberts. We didn't have chairs like they have now. It were forms,

St John's school, 1933, Class 3.

St John's school 1946-47. The teacher is Mr Cowling. Third row from front, second right is Pat Carthy (Mrs Pat Bolt).

and you all sat next to each other, and you'd talk to each other sometimes. There was this Miss Roberts – she lived in Town Lane, Dukinfield – and if she'd see anyone talking, she'd shout 'No talking! No talking!' I had an auntie who were a schoolteacher. She were at Moravian in Dukinfield. Miss Roberts shouted a time or two at me and she said, 'I'll see your auntie when I'm going home.' But it didn't bother me. We all had a book and a pencil and ink.

Miss Lily Birch

Getting strapped for Lizzie

When I were at Hob Hill, they used the strap. I had it once. I lived in Cheetham Hill Road. On my way down to school were what we called Booth Street. At the bottom end of Booth Street were a girl who used to sit next to me at school. I used to call for her every morning. When I called in her mother'd say, 'Oh, she'll only be a minute.' Well, she were above a minute. When we got to school we were late. So, 'Hold your hand out.' It were a proper big strap; you daren't move your hand and you got such a whack on it. So I told me mother I got strapped nearly every day. 'What for?' 'Being late.' 'Well, you go out of here soon enough.' 'I call for Lizzie.' 'Don't call for her again.' She made me go down High Street, so I wouldn't go down Booth Street.

Miss Lily Birch

Victoria Road infants, Dukinfield, in the 1920s

I started school, when I was five, at a little infants' school on Victoria Road; it was a day school during the week and a Sunday school on Sundays. I remember very, very vividly we used to count with beads. There was always one or the other one who got a bead fast up their nose; they used to see how far they could put it; then the lesson had to be stopped for it to be retrieved. That sticks in my mind, and the outside toilets that we had to do a little run to if it was wet. I remember a Miss Foreweather; she wasn't the head but she was a very plump, rounded lady.

Mrs Alice Edwards

Globe Lane school, Dukinfield, in the 1920s

I went from Victoria Road Infants to Globe Lane school. The head teacher was Mr Firth. I enjoyed it. All the subjects in those days were taught by one teacher and each year you had a different teacher. There was one man teacher there, but I can't remember his name. There was lady that taught the third year and she really was a tartar. Everybody was sort of aware of Katy – we called her Katy. I did have the cane twice there. She said it was for talking, and I was only listening. I was more embarrassed than anything. I didn't tell my parents I'd had the cane. The singing stands out in my mind. We used to stand in the biggest space there and had a teacher playing the piano. The school I went to is where Woodmet is now; they built a new school higher up the lane. When I went to Globe Lane school there was nothing there except the farm halfway down the lane – Kenworthy's farm. It was all fields. To go to the farm you had to go down about twenty steps. When you're young it was rather daunting. On the other side of the lane was a railway place – the Wagon Works. A lot of Dukinfield people worked at the Wagon Works; it took all of that stretch from the White Bridge down to Globe Square.

Mrs Alice Edwards

St Paul's school, Stalybridge, in the 1930s

The wonderful Miss Hassall

My first school was St Paul's school on Huddersfield Road, Stalybridge, right opposite St Paul's church. It was an infants and a junior school. It was there where I got my first grounding of Christianity. It's a Church of England school. We had Scripture every morning for half an hour. We had a good grounding. We learned the Catechism and the stories of the Bible. We had a headmistress, Miss Hassall; she taught me, she'd taught my mother and she taught my eldest daughter. She was a wonderful person. She actually ran a Sunday morning children's class, not so much as a Sunday school class – that was separate. She organized what was known as a Churchgoers' Guild. When I was six, I was asked if I wanted to go. Mother and father weren't churchgoing people, but they sent me and I joined the Churchgoers' Guild. She got a group of perhaps thirty to forty children in the church every Sunday morning and we got stamps to put in a book afterwards. I went to Sunday school in the afternoon.

Mr Tom Evans

A cup of milk

I started school at five years old and I went to St Paul's school on Huddersfield Road. It was a very happy school and I look back on it with very fond memories. There was no such thing in those days as free milk; if we wanted milk we used to have to take a penny a day; that meant halfpenny in the morning for a cup of milk and halfpenny in the afternoon. A local milkman used to come and fill our mugs of milk. Later on – I can't remember when – it used to come in little bottles with a little cardboard press-in top. When I started, in the very first class, I think we started with slates; then we went on to pencils and books; but we didn't have those in the first class.

Mrs Joyce Hall

A Christian person, a lovely lady

The headmistress at St Paul's was Miss Hassall. She had taught my mother. She was a Christian person, a lovely lady. I was the eldest of three; my father was out of work. Friday we used to take our milk money; it was tuppence-halfpenny a week for one bottle, five pence for two. My mother had given my brother five pence, my younger sister five pence, but, when it got to me, the oldest, she'd say, 'Will you only have one this week?' because she hadn't got the money until father came with a bit of money on Friday night. I'd say, 'Yes, it's all right.' She'd say, 'Well, you're the biggest, you're the strongest.' I'd go to school and Miss Hassall would take the register with the money. I'd go out and I'd say, 'One this week, Miss Hassall; my mum can't afford two.' She'd say, 'All right.' Then, just as we were going out to play, she'd come and she'd say, 'I've put the other two and a half pence in.' I'd go home and I'd tell my mum she'd paid for me, and my mum used to cry, because she was embarrassed. At that time nearly all the parents worked in the mills and the mills were going through a bad time; we were all pretty poor and there were a lot of poor children. Miss Hassall would ask some children if they'd go to tea at her house on a Saturday. None of them would go; I don't know why. I went. I used to go every Saturday. It was a long way up Huddersfield Road. We used to have tea together and she used to show me all her treasures. She had a lovely home, with all lovely things. Sometimes she'd say, 'If you'd like to come to church on

Sunday night, you can sit in my pew. She had a little pew at the front, which just held two. She'd let me sit in the front with her and oh! I was proud. The other children were making fun of me, but I loved her. She gave me a Panama hat. As I was coming out, she said, 'Put it on.' I said, 'No, I'll carry it.' She put me a banana in it. I carried it home and every Sunday I went to church with my panama hat; the other kids used to knock it off. But I loved it, and I loved her too. She lived to a good age; she was a well thought of old lady – only little, a tiny lady, a lovely lady.

Mrs Joyce Hall

St Paul's school in the 1940s

A typical school marm

I went to St Paul's school on Huddersfield Road. The teacher who sticks in my mind, who I think was the head teacher, was a Miss Hassall. She was a wonderful lady, very strict, but very kind. She was a good teacher; she had the knack of instilling knowledge without fear. She sticks out vividly in my mind – a typical school marm; very small, black stockings, long skirts, hair all scraped back with a little bob at the back, and very thin glasses; she used to wear them on the end of her nose and peer through. A wonderful woman!

Mr Ron Watkins

St James' day school, Millbrook

How long does this last?

I was born in 1905 and I started to go to school – St James' Day school – when I were three years old. We went full-time; no play school, like there is now. First day, when I came home, I says, 'How much longer have I

to go there?' I hated school. I loved needlework, sewing, anything like that, but as far as reading, writing – my mother said, 'Eh, you're going to be a right dunce, you.' I says, 'Well, I don't care. I can write my name.' The headmaster were Mr Hibbert, and the teachers were Fanny Hayes, Agnes Norris, Lizzie Roberts. They were very strict. Agnes Norris threw a piece of chalk at me once. I says, 'I shall tell my mother over you.' I did, and she said, 'You deserved it.' I were always in trouble. I was caned once for talking. Didn't tell my mother; she would have said, 'Serves you right!'

Mrs Alice Young

A painful lesson

I went to St James', Millbrook, in the second half of the 1930s. The headmaster was Mr Wood and there was a Mrs Martin among the teachers. She used to teach us to wash combs and brushes – I suppose that were supposed to be Domestic Science. They still had the cane when I went to school. You'd have the cane if you didn't get your sums right. It made you sit up and think, 'Well, if I don't get this right, I might have the cane again.' If you did anything wrong and you had the cane, you didn't do it again.

Mrs Margaret Green

Discrimination

I was born in Millbrook, on Huddersfield Road, on 22 August 1910. I started school at St James' school, which belonged to the Church of England. I can remember getting in trouble many a time. You got in trouble for talking. They used the cane, but only on the boys. They didn't cane the girls. That didn't go down very well with the boys. The head teacher was a man and he wouldn't cane the girls. I went to St James' till I was fourteen. My mother used to tell us that when she came from Wales to Stalybridge to live at first, she went to school and sometimes they'd have her stood up at the front talking. She talked Welsh and they were fascinated. Her Welsh soon went, but me grandad's didn't.

Mrs Gladys Heap

Castle Hall school, Stalybridge

Castle Hall school in 1915

When I was five, I went to Castle Hall school, which was just around the corner. The thing I remember most, one of the teachers tried to tell us about home-making and things. One week she made a big rice pudding in a tin. My mother took it home for her and cooked it. We all got a little bit of rice pudding. We

learned writing and arithmetic and sewing and knitting. In the infants' school we had slates and pencils; then when we moved up to Standard 1 you got pencil and paper. We wiped the slates with a cloth. The head teacher was Miss Walker; she was over the girls. Miss Dunlop was in the infants and Mr France was upstairs. Mr Morris was there a long time, then Mr France took over. They used the cane; girls used to get caned as well. I had the strap once, for being late.

Mrs May Redford

The teachers of Castle Hall school in the 1920s

I went to Castle Hall school. They turned out some good scholars. We'd a good headmaster. When I went to West Hill at eleven, they said, 'How've you got Geometry?' I said, 'We were

Castle Hall school, c. 1910. The teachers, from right to left, are Miss Lowe, Mrs Holt and Miss Lawton.

Castle Hall school, 1922, Infant's Class 1. The teachers are Miss Dunlop (left) and Miss Richardson (right).

taught it at Castle Hall.' They were annoyed; they said, 'Well, they've no right to teach it there, because you weren't old enough for it.' The headmaster were called Arthur Morris. He took us all down to th'art gallery in Manchester. We went down on the train and it were sixpence I paid, I think. Then we all trooped to th' theatre in library. He had a plot up Hough Hill and he used to take us up there and point out what he had in his garden and that. He told us all about the hills and moors of Stalybridge. When I went to Castle Hall school there were Miss Ashton – she taught top class; there were Miss Richardson, Miss Rawton. The headmistress, I don't know whether she were Miss or Mrs Dunlop. They were all in the infants. Then, when we were growing we went upstairs into top school – Miss Sheenan, Mrs Chollerton, Harold Shaw and one whose name I can't remember. Later

a chap called Stokes come. Then there were a chap called France. He taught Standard 7. I finished up in Standard 7 when I were eleven. I were with lads older than me, because I were a good scholar really.

Mr Percy Norton

Castle Hall school during the Second World War

I went to Castle Hall school and I hated it. The headmaster was Harry France, known as 'Cocky' France. They were too strict. I could understand that you got in trouble for talking in proper lessons, like English and History, but I couldn't understand why, when you were sewing, in the sewing class, you got strapped if you talked.

Mr John Perry

Mrs Ashworth and the Rising Moon

One of the teachers was Mrs Ashworth and I thought she was lovely. She lived in a flat on Mottram Road. I remember getting in trouble with my mother over Mrs Ashworth. At weekends, if the weather was nice, we used to go a walk up Hough Hill. There was a pub up there – still is – the Rising Moon on Matley Lane. If it was a nice night we always sat outside and my dad brought a drink out, lemonade for me, shandy for me mother. Mrs Ashworth was giving us a lesson one day, and said, 'There's a public house on Matley Lane; I can't remember whether it's called the Rising Moon or the Rising Sun.' So, of course, Jean puts her hand up and says, 'It's the Rising Moon, Mrs Ashworth; we go there at weekends.' I couldn't understand why my mother was cross with me. We had lads in our class, and they were terrors really. We had two bright sparks and they used to wee in the inkwells.

Mrs Jean Pilling

Old St George's school, Stalybridge, c. 1915

I started to go to school when I was five in 1915. I went to Old St George's school. It's a nursing home now. The headmaster was Mr Hayes. We used to have slates to write on with slate pencils. If we wanted to rub anything out we just used a cloth. The piece of slate had

Castle Hall school, 1925, Standard 6. Front row, third from right, Percy Norton aged ten.

Jack and the Beanstalk. Castle Hall school, 1952.

wood around it. Later on we had exercise books. There wasn't one scholar leaving school who couldn't read – which doesn't happen today, does it?

Mrs Nellie Howarth

West Hill boys' school, Stalybridge

A smashing draughtsman!

I went to West Hill boys' school in 1926, when I were eleven. I started off in 1A, and then I went in 2A and then I got double pneumonia when I were twelve. I were off school and never did any exams. So I went into 3B. After I left school, the chap that did Geometry – Ashworth were his name; tragically he died young; he were a nice chap – saw me wheeling

a barrow, coming from the station. 'What are you doing?' he says. I said, 'I'm tripe dressing.' 'Good God,' he says, 'you'd have made a smashing draughtsman. Your drawings and plans and elevations were spot on; they were perfect.' 'Well,' I said, 'why did you always keep giving me 90 out of 100?' 'Because,' he said, 'you wouldn't have tried any more if I had a' done. You'd have been too cocky.'

Mr Percy Norton

West Hill boys' school, late 1930s and early '40s

I went to West Hill. That was a good school. I was lucky enough to be in the A form all the way through. Some of the lads from that class did really well for themselves. One lad called Sidebottom held the chair of Humanities at

Christchurch University, New Zealand. The teachers were all men, eleven men, and one woman. The woman was Mrs Gill. They were all good teachers, but very strict. The headmaster was Mr Fletcher.

Mr Tom Evans

Rounding up the runaways

At West Hill in the summer we had the masters versus the scholars cricket match one afternoon. That was a compulsory event – we had to watch. One or two, being lads, slipped away a bit early. Mr Fletcher saw them go. He jumped on a cycle, with his cane, and rounded them up, chased them back to school, like a cowboy rounding up runaway cattle.

Mr Tom Evans

Six of the best

I was at West Hill Boys' school during the war. I ought to remember the headmaster's name; he gave me six of the best. To go to school from where we lived, we used to cut through the goods yard, then up Station Brew to West Hill. In the goods yard on one side there was the river. There was some sets that had been put there from one of the roads that had been dug up. We were rolling some of these sets down, to make ports at the side of the river. The foreman of the yard caught us and reported us to the headmaster. He called us out by our names and called us 'saboteurs'. He said he would punish us for what we'd done. We got six of the best on each hand. He always got it timed that he got the cane, a very thin one, right across your fingers. It brought tears to

Technical school, Waterloo Road, Stalybridge. It became the Central school for girls. The building is now used as a resources centre.

your eyes. He was only a small bloke, but he had it marked out where he could stand and where you could stand. You put your hand out and you had it there, across the tips of your fingers. When you got back to your classroom, your hands were dead. The teacher didn't bother; they knew what had happened, and left you alone until the feeling came back.

Mr Bob Sleigh

West Hill Boys' school, late 1940s

I went to West Hill in 1946. I remember some of the teachers quite well. We had a maths teacher called Bill Heapy, who was a soft touch. He used to take us for Maths and Religious Knowledge. We were an irreverent lot, because nobody was interested much in Religious Knowledge. We used to get him talking about football – get him talking about Stalybridge Celtic and you'd cracked it. Into the second chapter of Isaiah, and somebody'd start talking about how badly Celtic did on Saturday and that was it until the bell went. Then he'd play hell. 'You've done it again, haven't you? Got me talking about football!' Harry Jones was the History teacher. There was a P.T. (Physical Training) teacher – I can't remember his name – but he used to wield a mean plimsoll across your backside if you misbehaved. I've had 'Dunlop' written on me bum more than once! There was a man called Cecil Browning who taught Geography. He had at some time been in Africa, and he used to have this assegai in the corner of his classroom and was very fond of talking about it. Then there was Joe Lowe, a real character. Harry Baxter was the Woodwork teacher. He was a bit of a tartar. The minute he left the room, we'd all be making guns to fire match stalks. He used to confiscate them all when he came back, if he caught us doing it.

Mr Ron Watkins

Lakes Road Girls' school when it opened in 1932.

Lakes Road girls' school, 1933, first year. Third row back, third from right is Betty Taylor (Mrs Betty Jones).

Lakes Road Girls' school, Dukinfield

Mrs Wood and Miss Ashton

I went to Lakes Road school when it opened. The headmistress was Mrs Wood; she had a bungalow up on Werneth Low, and, in our turns, each class used to walk up to Werneth Low. She had big long gardens and we used to take our sandwiches with us and she'd give us lemonade. We used to spend the afternoon there and then we'd walk back. Miss Ashton lived at a farm, and she used to take the children up to the farm sometimes. Also, when we went to the baths, we had to go to

Ashton, because Dukinfield didn't have its own baths then. We used to cross over the canal and go that way to Ashton baths.

Miss Annice Ritson

Lakes Road staff in the early 1940s

I started at Lakes Road in 1940. The headmistress was Mrs Wood. She got a medal, an MBE or OBE. She went to Buckingham Palace for it. I remember, when she came back, she told us about it and about meeting the King. Mrs Andrew was the Art teacher; Miss Ashton taught History; Mrs Jackson was Geography; Miss Norris and Miss Fidler used

St Mark's school, 1925. Front row, second from right is Harry Greenhalgh, whose family had a sweetshop opposite the Princess cinema, Dukinfield.

to take sport and do Domestic Science, and I think Miss Fidler used to take Maths as well. Miss Titterington took Needlework and Miss Lodge took Music. There was two classrooms upstairs and Miss Lodge had one. When we were finishing school for the holidays, they used to say how many merits you had. In Art lessons, when it was nice, they used to take you out and you sat at a tree and y'had to draw the tree – a lot better than being stuck in the classroom. I was thrilled to bits when we got the uniform; it was navy blue and yellow.

Mrs Ethel Gee

A tale of three gooseberries

I went to Lakes Road when I was eleven years old in 1943. We never spent much time in the classrooms. They built air-raid shelters at the side of the hockey pitch. I built the steps to go up onto the hockey pitch. We used to grow vegetables up there. We had garden plots where we used to grow cabbages and potatoes and things like that. The headmistress was Mrs Wood. After Mrs Wood there was Miss Wilson, who was deputy head until Mrs Wood retired. Mrs Wood was very small, and very strict. I got into trouble with her. I stole three gooseberries and put them in a tin. The gooseberry bush was encroaching on my steps

Central school for girls, Stalybridge, 1929, Class 4. Second row from back, extreme right is Gladys Bardsley (Mrs Percy Norton).

Central school for girls, Stalybridge, 1947. Class 3A.

and I decided to break off some of the branches. I put the three gooseberries in a tin and put it in my pocket. I was spotted and called to Mrs Wood's room. Blow me, there was a policeman there. He was a community policeman who used to live on Pickford Lane. I had to turn my pockets out. I didn't know what I'd done. They opened this tin and three gooseberries fell out. I got order marks, which counted against your house. The houses were Masefield, which had a yellow badge; Milne, which was blue; Hardy, which was green and Newbolt, which was red. It was a very serious thing when you got an order mark. At the end of term you were in assembly; you were all sat down and those with order marks had to stand up; you disgraced the house.

Mrs Vera Win Hotchkiss

Lakes Road school, late 1940s-early '50s

I went to Lakes Road in 1948 when I was eleven. The headmistress was Miss Wilson. You walked on the other side of the road if you saw Miss Wilson. Miss Ashton was the History teacher; Mr Dutton taught shorthand and typing; Mr Bentley, the Science teacher, would throw the board duster at you if you misbehaved, and he'd flick the chalk. The school was like an E-shape; lovely big playing fields at the back. There was a shower block, which the boys from Crescent Road school used to share with us. One lot had to get out before the other lot could get in.

Mrs Pat Bolt

4 People and Places

My father – a proud man

Between 1932 and 1939 my dad was out of work. He wasn't on his own and we never felt poor because everyone was in the same boat. He used to walk miles and miles looking for work. He was a member of the committee of the Conservative Club and he had a friend who was a big window cleaner; he cleaned the windows of the infirmary and that. He said to my dad, 'I'll give you a job, Jim.' Dad started and the first job he had was to clean the windows of a house. He went up, but then he said, 'I can't come down.' He told them to knock on the door and ask the lady to open the window and let him in. His friend said to him once, 'I've paid your subs; you're all right going down to the club.' My dad said, 'I'll go when I've got a job.' 'No, you're all right,' said his friend. 'Look, I know I'd be all right.

Opening of Dukinfield Town Hall.

You'd buy me a pint, Luke'd buy me a pint, Sam would buy me a pint, and I couldn't buy you one back. No, it's not on.' He had a friend along the road, a widower. Every day he'd go looking for jobs; every evening he'd go down to his friend's. They used to sit playing dominoes or cards. They used to send our Alice to the little corner shop for a ha'penny packet of Lyon's cocoa. They'd put it in a pint pot and put sugar in it, but no milk. That's what they used to do, and my dad liked a pint.

Mrs Ethel Anderson

Beyond Cheetham Hill Road

There were none of these houses up here when I were a kid. All this was fields and farms. Where my garden is, we used to sit

there. A path went through to another farm and there were a farm on the other side. In summer, when it were nice, a lot of girls – there was a lot of girls where I lived – would get a basket of something to eat and we used to go across to the farm for some milk. Across there were the reservoir; we used to climb up the wall and look in the reservoir.

Miss Lily Birch

Miss Waite and her dog

In the late 1930s–early 1940s, when I was a kid, beyond Cheetham Hill Road it was all fields. Right at the top of Yew Tree Lane there used to be a single-decker bus. It used to be the headquarters for the Dukinfield Home Guard. My dad used to go up there; they had

Astley grammar school staff, c. 1962. Miss Daphne Waite is the headmistress. The compiler of this book is sixth from the left, second row from the back.

Ashorth's Restaurant, Stalybridge. Leonard Ashworth is in the doorway.

a great view. I remember them building the houses on Chester Avenue. I can remember them building the old people's home, Yew Trees, where my mother went to be seamstress. I also remember them building Astley Grammar School for Girls. Miss Daphne Waite was Astley's first headmistress, and she had a little dog, Tuppence, that went everywhere with her. I can see her now, with that dog, trotting across from the school to Cliff's paper shop.

Mrs Pat Bolt

'Going down into the wood'

Cheetham Hill Road hasn't altered much since I were a child in the early part of the last century. There was a little shop that sold all sorts. There was a post office, which sold bits of haberdashery. There was a field; well, it was a tip, a small tip. There was a little pond there, on th'end of the Rope Works. John Taylor's Rope Works were at the back. There was a pond, where the school is built now. There was a passageway; they used to call it, 'Going down into the wood.' I don't know why, because there was no wood there. We used to call John Taylor Johnny Bant. 'I'm going to Johnny Bant's.'

Mr Alex Cox

My dad the cobbler

My dad was in France during the First World War. While he was away my mother had buried a daughter, Annie. When dad came home he used to repair a lot of shoes for the neighbours. His father had taught him how to do it, and he taught our Frederick how to do it. He said, 'Some day it'll come in handy for you.' Anyway, eventually my dad got a little shop in Ashton, near Trafalgar Square. It were only very small, like a little hut shop. My brother and I used to go all the way to take him his dinner. Mum would put it in a little basin – she'd done potato pie or something – and we'd go all the way along Wharf Street, King Street, Victoria Street to Trafalgar Square to take it to him. He was a very good cobbler; he made clogs as well. He always used to put the nails in his mouth. A lady said to me the other day, 'Your father always used to make my husband's shoes. He was a smart man'. That was nice, wasn't it?

Mrs Betty Jones

Picking for coal in Coalpit Hills

The Astley Pit was in Dukinfield. It closed eventually, but, as they did in those days, they left these mounds of slag all over the place. For us kids, of course, it was somewhere to play – 'Cowboys and Indians', 'English and Germans' (only nobody wanted to be Germans). We used to go on the Coalpit Hills, as we called them. When there was trouble with the mines and nearly everybody was out of work, soon after the First World War, with all the soldiers coming back, we used to go 'picking' for coal. I can remember the little coal rake now, a little iron coal rake it were, raking among the slag at the top – 'Ooh, a piece of coal!' It was worth going for. That was one way in which you eased the burden of living.

Mr David Cooper

My mother

I was born in Kay Street in Castle Hall in 1910. My mother lived in that same house for sixty-eight years. We had a neighbour, Mrs Brownlow, who lived next door but one. She looked after my mother when she had her children and mother looked after Mrs Brownlow when she had hers. My mother

used to befriend little lads. One lad, John Turner, lived round the corner. He used to take papers and, when he came back, he always come to our house and he had a toast and a pint of tea before he went home. He died on that submarine that went down in Liverpool, the *Thetis*, was it? There was another lad who lived at the bottom of our yard; we lived at the top. When our Marjorie were growing up, she used to take my dad's dinner; Jimmy Wellman took his dad's and they used to go together. They always had a roasted potato to go with; my mother did Jimmy one an'all. Another lad, Ron Jones, lived lower down. His mother died and he was always in our house. She was always kind to little lads.

Mrs May Redford

The Cottage of Content

As you go along High Street towards Dukinfield, Quarry Street is on your left. Years ago there was a big mill, Robert Platt's, on the right as you went up Quarry Street, and Christ Church (that's gone now) was on your left. There were a few cottages before you got to Christ Church. In the middle of them was a public house, not much bigger than the cottages themselves; it was called the Cottage of Content. There were cottages on the opposite side as well, which belonged to the mill.

Mrs Nellie Howarth

Looking after mother

My mother had her foot off when she was only a girl. She worked at Clasher's on Tame Valley. Trams used to run down there in those days. The tram would come along Tame Valley and up Wharf Street and stop at the Queen's Arms. There was a local joke – 'Where was your husband last night?' 'In the

Queen's Arms.' I used to get up first to get things going at home and to take me mother down to the tram, because, especially in wet weather, icy weather, foggy weather, she didn't stand a chance of getting to the tram. Once she got on the tram, of course, they'd look after her; that's how we were brought up. I was up at five o'clock in the morning, before the knocker-up. We had knockers-up in those days, tap, tap, tap. When mother was coming home I had to go and meet her and bring her home. I'd get the dinner ready first.

Mr David Cooper

My mother the centenarian

My mother used to go out cleaning, just for a bit of extra money. I thought this was hard work because she didn't get much money. If I had any money, sometimes I'd put it in her purse, put a penny or two in her purse, to help. When a job came at the district bank, on the corner of Chapel Street and King Street, she came down here. She worked at the bank until she retired. In fact, I put her notice in when she was seventy – 'It's time you packed up.' She was 102 when she died. She was as bright as a button. Even at church people said, 'Your mother puts us to shame, the way she goes in the kitchen and washes up.' She came to work at the bank as a cleaner-caretaker. She had started work part-time at thirteen, and she had to walk from Dukinfield to Stalybridge every day. They had coal fires, and they had to light the fire so they could brew a cup of tea before they went to work.

Mr Kenneth Gee

Tame Valley in the 1940s

When I was a child there were a lot of mills in Tame Valley – Bowker and Ball's, Tower Mill, the Old Mill, Park Road Mill. That's four I

can think of offhand. They were all cotton mills. Then there was the cooperage, and the brewery and Holderness', the cleaners, and there was a sheet metal works and Potter's insulation. A lot of people rarely went off the valley. They lived there and worked there; their friends and their social life was there. I think you'd be hard put to find anyone who lives and works in the valley now. Then it was a lifelong thing. Me mum had been a child in our house and still lived and worked in the valley in the same house when she was eighty. She wasn't exceptional; there were a lot like her.

Mrs Barbara Perry

The blind pianist in the Minder's Arms

I used to go to the Minder's Arms to get a jug of beer for my mother. They knew what I was going for, and they used to allow me to go in. In those days there used to be a lot of entertainment, just from a piano, in a pub. There was a lady who used to play the piano in the Minder's Arms and she was completely blind. Being interested in music, I would spend a quarter of an hour, twenty minutes, in there. I'd say, 'Don't pull the beer yet. I'm just going to have a listen.' I'd just listen to this lady playing; she was quite good. I met her years and years later, when I started playing in a dance band. I saw her at a place where we played, and I thought, 'I know that lady.'

Mr John Perry

Ashworth's restaurant

My uncle Leonard and auntie Sarah had a restaurant in Stalybridge – Ashworth's restaurant, not far from Holy Trinity church. The restaurant was very nice; they used to have really lovely meat and potato pie. I spent a lot

Mrs Alice Carthy (mother of Mrs Pat Bolt) at the back of her home on Lodge Lane. Cheetham Hill Road is at the back.

An unusual publican

I had an uncle who won some money on the football pools. The war was on. He asked my mum and dad if they'd like him to buy them a pub. Neither mum nor dad drank, but dad was in a job which was ruining his health; so they said yes. So he bought them a village pub called the Grapes in Heyrod. We lived there for seventeen years. My father was a character. He wouldn't let anybody come in the pub if they swore; he actually turned them out and banned a lot of people. He wouldn't let anybody play cards, which was what they used to do in taprooms. He was a very strict man, but a good publican, and was well respected for it. You'd have thought he'd have lost customers, but I think they came to look at him because he was an oddity. A lady come in and she said, 'Don't let our — have too much to drink tonight, Albert; only I've got to buy shoes for the children in the morning.' He said, 'Right,' and when he thought that he had had enough, he said, 'You've got to go home now, because you've got to buy shoes in the morning.' He wasn't a bit like you'd expect a publican to be.

Mrs Joyce Hall

of time there. They had something unusual: a bathroom. When my uncle Leonard died very suddenly, they never rang the bells at Holy Trinity until after his funeral. When they rang the bells you could hear them in every room in Ashworth's. They hadn't a clock anywhere in the place because everywhere you went you could see the market clock. I used to go and play in these rooms at the top, where they didn't know what I was getting up to. Anybody will remember Ashworth's. After uncle Leonard died, auntie couldn't carry on; she couldn't pay all the bills there. So she opened a restaurant on Melbourne Street, just a little one, that took on making meals during the war. Ashworth's had been a hotel as well.

Mrs Gladys Heap

Lobby houses of Rose Terrace

I was born in 1910 in Rose Terrace, Stalybridge, which backs onto the canal. The houses are quite old; they must be well over a hundred years old, though they have been renovated. They'd three rooms downstairs and two rooms up. They were lobby houses. Downstairs they'd a front room, a living room and a kitchen, two bedrooms upstairs and a bit of a garden at the back. On a canal there's only one towpath, isn't there. We didn't have the towpath; we were at the other side. The back door came to the canal and the front door faced the church.

Mrs Nellie Howarth

The Eastwood family. The baby is six-month-old Joyce Kay (Mrs Joyce Hall). Albert Kay, her father, 'the unusual publican' is second from the left on the back row

My grandad

My grandfather was sort of a local character. He worked at more or less everything. He was a coal miner and worked at the pit in Dukinfield called Astley Deep. When they shut it down because it became unsafe, he moved to the Snipe pit. He used to say that the Snipe was known as the 'One a day' pit, because, on average, one man a day was killed there. He left the mine and he went working at a factory in Ryecroft in Ashton, where they made explosives during the 1914–1918 war. It set on fire. My grandfather and his brother got out safely, but they went back for somebody. His brother and the other man got out, but me grandad was blown out, through the windows. He got very badly burned and had no ears; his ears had gone. His face was very, very badly

scarred, and his hands were crippled. The sinews and tendons had been so badly damaged that, although he could straighten his hands, they flicked back again. He decided to get a light job when he recovered, and he went working for a stonemason called Sid Wild at the bottom of Huddersfield Road in Stalybridge. His job was to go out, winter and summer, round all the local graveyards, Stalybridge, Mottram church, the whole area, with a bucket and some cleaning cloths and stones and scrubbers and clean all the gravestones that Sid Wild had installed. He did this all year, in middle of winter, a bucket of cold water, ice everywhere, scrubbing gravestones. One of my memories, as a little lad, is of sitting there in the morning at the side of the fire before he went to work. There was some ointment in those days, called Snowfire

Astley Pit.

Ointment. It was a little green block in a yellow carton with a picture of a fire on. I used to sit there and he used to let me warm this ointment at the side of the fire and then fill all the cracks in his fingers with it. He couldn't move his fingers; the skin was so tender you could see the bones inside his fingers. He used to let me fill the little holes in with this Snowfire ointment and then he'd go and clean gravestones all day, in the middle of winter. That to him was a light job. He was a very hard man, but a gentler man you could never wish to meet.

Mr Ron Watkins

Pantomime steps

When I was eleven, in 1933, I went to Lakes Road girls' school. That was just off Pickford Lane and a long way to walk from Tame Valley. You walked along Tame Valley, up Tower Street and it brought you to Pantomime Brew. There were quite a lot of steps, the kind that curved around. We thought nothing of going up them as children. You had to go that way or walk all the way around the river. It was very lonely, so a friend and I always went together. My grandad and grandma Taylor were on the way, so sometimes I used to pop in their house.

Mrs Betty Jones

If you walked from the Oxford cinema, down Sandy Lane, to get to Tower Street you had to walk down all these very, very steep stone steps. There were sand-hills at one side. There must have been about fifty of these steps. They ran down by the cemetery wall on Tower Street. They were called Pantomime Steps.

Mrs Pat Bolt

Will Wally cry?

At Wellington Street Methodist church they always had a Christmas pantomime. One time a lad named Wally – his real name was Walter – had a poem to say. All the mothers and grandmothers sat there wondering, 'Will Wally say his poem, or will he cry? What will happen?' Well, Wally didn't cry, but the mothers and grandmothers did. He stood up and he said, 'When I were young and in me prime, I could eat a muffin anytime. But now I'm old and getting grey, it takes me nearly half a day.' They all called 'Encore!' So on he comes again. Only a little fat thing he were.

Mr David Cooper

The Drill Hall

Up in Castle Hall was the Drill Hall. I think it was the Cheshire Regiment. Occasionally they'd have such a thing as a travelling circus there. I remember going as a child when one came. Of course that was at one end. At the other end was a couple of guns.

Mr Tom Evans

A kind employer

When I left school in 1949 I went to work at Thompson and Cooke Solicitors, in Stamford Street, Stalybridge. After I got married I wanted to work part-time and they didn't employ part-timers. I went to Mr Cooke and said that I'd have to give my notice in. He asked me if I'd like to work Mondays, Tuesdays and Wednesdays, which suited me. My mother later had a massive heart attack, and he sent for me. I'd been up to see her; she was at home – they wouldn't move her to hospital because she was too ill. He said, 'You go home now, Jean, and I don't want to see you again until your mother's on the mend.' I

Adamson' Band in Dukinfield Park, 1937. The town hall is at the back.

Whit Walks crossing King Street onto Astley Street, c. 1930. The Commercial pub is on the right and George Mason, grocer, is in the background.

Second Ashton, later first Stalybridge, Guide Group in Cheetham's Park, c. 1945.

said, 'Mr Cooke, I can't; I've got three books of shorthand and I don't think anybody can read mine.' He told me, 'I don't care if you've got thirty-three books of shorthand. That can wait. You go home and you see to your mother.' Not many bosses would do that.

Mrs Jean Pilling

Astley Street church

When I was a child during the First World War, we were Primitive Methodists and we went to Astley Street church. That was a sitting target for the explosion that happened in Ashton. After the explosion there wasn't much left, only the walls; all the windows were blown through. As lads, we thought, 'Well, chapel's gone. We don't have to go now.' I wasn't reckoning on my dad. He said, 'We're having the service outside. So you're going.' I sat as far as I could from the front, but I was there. They had these open-air services for quite a long time, until they got things under control. I can remember this drawing at home of the front of the church; every brick and stone was numbered. You could buy a brick or stone or window, so that it could be built up again.

Mr David Cooper

A true Christian

When my dad kept the Grapes pub in Heyrod, I used to wait on in the evenings, until I got married. On a Friday night, my mum used to make sandwiches, and we used to have a man come in to play the piano and have a little sing-song. There was never anything nasty. I've seen more Christianity in a pub, in a taproom, than I've ever seen in a church. I've seen lots of kind deeds done by people who enjoy a pint. We were right near the power station and we used to have a lot of London men come in who worked for the London Electricity Board. I remember one night a crowd of men came in who were working at the power station. The boss came in later and he shouted one of them out. He said, 'You're sacked. Pick your cards up when you go back.' Everything went quiet and the boss walked out. All the other men started to talk. 'You haven't done it. He did it.' One of them said, 'He did it; I'll go and tell the boss.' 'No, don't,' he said. When I was serving him, I said, 'Have you got sacked and it's somebody else's fault?' He said, 'Well, he's got three children, and I've none.' He got sacked from his job because he was thinking of the other man. Now that, to me, was a true Christian act.

Mrs Joyce Hall

Thomas Hope, publishers

In 1934, when I was fourteen, I left school. I went to work at Thomas Hope, an educational publisher on Chapel Street, at the back of London Road (now Piccadilly) station in Manchester. The Hopes owned it and one of them, Sidney, was an MP. There were three or four brothers. They supplied all the schools with books. Sidney Hope always used to get theatre tickets given to him free, and he always used to give them to the workpeople. So we got to see all the plays and different things that were on in Manchester. Although it was what was called a non-union place, Mr Hope would pay for people to go to the dentist and opticians and he always gave Christmas boxes, which a lot of firms didn't.

Miss Annice Ritson

Barbara Castle and potato pie

I've been interested in politics since I was fifteen. Barbara Castle was secretary of the Labour Party League of Youth in Stalybridge

Guides assembled on Stalybridge market ground. The building on the right is the old baths.

and Hyde constituency. She's older than me and I was the youngster on the committee from Stalybridge. While she was the local MEP she used to come out and go round the town. She always hoped that she'd come to our house for potato pie. She'd kick her shoes off, sit on the settee and have a potato pie, which my wife had made.

Mr James Wainwright

Preserving the Hippodrome

The Hippodrome, on Corporation Street in Stalybridge, was apparently one of the oldest cinemas in the country. When I was foreman joiner for Stalybridge Council, the local borough surveyor was a man called Saville, who was a great believer in keeping traditions

alive and keeping original buildings as best he could. At the time the Hippodrome had been knocked down, but the frontage was still there. It badly needed repair. We had great discussions, him and I. I tended to go with him; I believed in keeping traditional buildings as they were. I was a young man then, and I could see the beauty of old buildings. We costed whether it would be viable to renew all the frontage – all the timberwork, all the great big box guttering, all the lead gutters. We costed it and decided it would be worth doing for posterity. This we did; we completely renewed it all, and its still there to this day. All the frontage of that cinema is still there, and I'm responsible. I'm proud of that.

Mr Ron Watkins

Stalybridge Town Hall.

Stalybridge Whit Walks 1952. The market hall is on the left, Holy Trinity church is behind the banner.

Saved by Billy Monks

When I was at school in 1947, my sister was at the same school, Stalybridge Central for Girls, and a lad named Jack Leach went to West Hill. There was a bad night, and, when we got off the bus in Millbrook, we could hardly lift our heads up, it were blizzarding that bad. We had to walk home. We went across the banking. The reservoir was at one side, and there was a big, steep wall there, and we went along that. As we turned the corner, there was the pump house. We got behind the wall there. Could we get going again? We couldn't. At that time Billy Monks, who had the garage in Ashton, had a big mansion at the top. I think it used to belong to the waterworks. As luck would have it, he picked us up and took us to the bottom of the lane. If not, I don't know how we'd have got home. We didn't go to school then for a day or two because of the snow; we used to sledge instead.

Mrs Margaret Green

The way through the fog

During the war I worked at an engineering works in Openshaw. One day it was very, very foggy. I thought, 'I'm never going to get home, all that way from Openshaw to Dukinfield. And I can't walk all the way around the valley, by the river, on me own.' I've always been a bit nervous. Anyway, there were twin sisters working with me who also came from Dukinfield. They said, 'We'll walk home together.' So we linked each other, walking through Openshaw to Dukinfield. It's a good walk that, through Ashton. We had to keep feeling the kerb. We got to Dukinfield and they said, 'We'll come your way.' So they came along Tame Valley with me. Then they had to go up Sandy Lane, onto Foundry Street and down into Parliament Street. They

actually came a long way around with me; it was very kind of them. But it was thick with fog. Every time you touched yourself, it was black. It was really dirty, foul!

Mrs Betty Jones

Brilliant fellow!

For a time when I was a child we lived down Guide Bridge, in Martin Street, in a big detached house. My brother and I went to St Stephen's school. What a tremendous headmaster! Oh, he was wonderful! He was called Albert, or Alfred, Taylor and he lived on Lakes Road in Dukinfield. He was a brilliant fellow. He used to keep the bright ones behind at four o'clock and give them extra tuition. There were about eight of us. I sat the exam to go to grammar school and I passed for Ashton Grammar. I went until I was fifteen; then I was removed by my parents, because they wanted me to stay at home.

Mrs Joyce Travis

The lady at Sykes' Ironmongery

When I was an apprentice at Copley Mill, I remember being sent to a firm called Sykes' Ironmongery, in Stalybridge. I have a vivid memory of a lady who worked there, a great big lady. I've no idea what she was called, but whatever you asked for, she knew exactly where it was. If you wanted some obscure fitting, nail, screw, tool, she would know exactly where to find it. She'd get the ladders and she'd shin up these ladders like a little monkey. She must have weighed best part of fifteen stone, but she was fit, really fit. She'd be up and down the ladders, blowing tons of dust off a cardboard box – you couldn't see for the dust – and inside would be what you wanted. I used to walk it from Copley Mill into Stalybridge and then carry the stuff back again

Mr John Mason, gamekeeper (father of Mrs Margaret Green). The reservoir is Higher Swineshaw. The farm, now demolished, is North Britain.

Joyce Hassall (Mrs Joyce Travis) with her mother, her grandmother Drury and her auntie, who lived in Bohemia Cottages.

to the mill. If it was really heavy, they'd allow me to take the handcart; anything above six pounds of nails they let me take the handcart. They didn't trust me with it very often.

Mr Ron Watkins

A politician or two

When Hugh Gaitskell was leader of the Labour Party, he once visited Stalybridge. I went along to the station to meet him. As we were walking along Market Street – we were just passing the White House – he started to tell me what his speech was. I says to him,

'The best thing you can do is be off to Leeds, if you're coming with that'. As a matter of fact, he used what I said as his speech. The following week George Brown went to the Princess Cinema in Dukinfield. I knew George Brown. I also knew Harold Wilson. I think he was the best Prime Minister we've ever had, a very clever man. He came to Stalybridge to open the Labour Club officially. I've met Neil Kinnock a few times; he's been a firebrand, but, like all of us, he's had the corners knocked off. I think he was an honest man with a good wife.

Mr James Wainwright

An advertisement for Sykes Ironmongery.

5 Work

Getting a job in t'mill

I left school at thirteen in 1918, and I couldn't get a job for a while. There was a girl I'd always been pals with, same age as me; we used to go everywhere together. We went on Tame Valley because all the mills were down there. We went to River Mill; my friend, Annie, knew somebody who worked there. We couldn't do anything, but we got in. The man who were boss said, 'Yes, I could do with two young girls. You go with that young woman over there, and you go to that one. They'll teach you everything.' They taught us 'reeling'. There was this machine that made hanks, not of wool, but of cotton and silk. It was a quiet room. I don't know how long I worked there, but we used to come home for us dinner. One day, when I were having dinner, knock came on t'door and a man shouted, 'Annie' (that were my mother) 'don't send that girl of yours back to work this afternoon.' My mother says, 'Why? What's she done?' 'She hasn't done anything,' he shouts. 'Doctor won't pass her. Says she has to go and have her tonsils out.'

Miss Lily Birch

Fifty-two years in t'mill

In 1917, when I were twelve years old, I went working in t'mill, in the cardroom. I used to do mornings from six o'clock until dinner-time at half-past twelve and then school in the afternoon. The next week it were school in the morning and mill in the afternoon. I did that for twelve months and then I went to work full-time. Then it was six o'clock in morning till half-past five at night. We had a dinner hour and what they called a 'breakfast half-hour' from half-past seven till eight o'clock in the morning. Dinnertime were from half-past twelve till half-past one; I went home for dinner 'cos I only lived down the street. The mill was Crookbottom Weaving; I had two machines. When I worked mornings I got 8s 6d a week; afternoons I got 7s 6d a week, but I had to work Saturday mornings. There was a whole gang of us girls. I wore clogs and black stockings but I would never wear a shawl. Mother'd say, 'Put that shawl on your head,' but I'd say, 'I'm not having a shawl; I'm only two minutes from my work.' The work weren't heavy, but it were tedious. I worked in one mill or another until I were sixty-five.

Mrs Alice Young

A sad way to get a job

My father worked in the mill and my mother worked in the mill. When I left school in the early 1920s I went to work in the mill. I couldn't get in at first, because it was only a small woollen mill, with just so many working there. When they'd been stopped a week, they had to go down the following week for their money. They'd have to come up to Millbrook,

Adshead's Mill (Bottomley's Cotton Waste Merchants).

turn round, go up the Ditchcroft, and go that way. They always went down by the canal. One particular day was very foggy. When you get down to the canal, just as you get into Stalybridge, you have to turn. There were three women walking together. They went in the water and two were drowned. That was when I got a job at the mill.

Mrs Gladys Heap

Working in t'mill in 1930s

It was hard work in the mill. I worked in the card-room and I had to look after two long frames with two hundred spindles on each. There were four hundred bobbins on each frame, which were coming through all the time. If a lump came in the cotton, you had to stop the frame because it snarled up. Then you had to piece it up and away it went. The bobbins were revolving all the time and, as

they came empty, I had to renew them with fresh bobbins. We couldn't have the windows open because it affected the running of the yarn. I've worked at ninety degrees in that cotton mill, but we took it in our stride. I started at 10s a week; then I went to 17s. The most wage I ever got in the mill, which was during the war, was 31s a week, of forty-eight hours.

Mrs Nellie Howarth

Retirement? What's that?

My mum, from being thirteen, worked in the cotton mills, part-time and then full-time; she did half school, then half mill work at the start. For many years she worked at Bowker & Ball's. They had no discrimination of any kind, including age discrimination. If you wanted to work and you could do the job, you had a job at Bowker & Ball's. My mum was

A mill-weaving shed decorated for a celebration.

still working there when she was eighty. She had been really happy there, and there were quite a few people like my mum, who were way over retirement age, but still wanted to work. At Bowker & Ball's they had a job as long as they wanted it.

Mrs Barbara Perry

Weaving at Leach's Mill

In 1925, when I was fifteen, I left school and went weaving at Leach's Mill. To start with I had two looms, then three; I didn't get to four before they closed down. I started work at 7.45 a.m. and finished at 5.30 p.m., and worked till noon on Saturdays. I earned about 10s a loom, so, with three looms, I got about 30s a week. I didn't like it at all, and I hated the clogs I had to wear.

Mrs May Redford

Lather boy

When I was fourteen, in 1924, I left school. I had been taking dinners for the spinners in the mill. I got one penny per day, plus a penny extra, which made it 6d a week. I carried two dinners, so I got 12d a week, which doesn't sound much but it was a good help to the family. Then I heard that a barber on King Street, Adam Oldfield, needed someone. I worked there on a Wednesday evening, a Friday evening and all day Saturday. I was a lather boy. I'd do the lathering, rubbing the soap in their faces. He'd do the shaving. If he was haircutting, I had a little shovel and a sweeping brush and kept the place looking tidy. I wasn't tall enough to reach their faces, so they gave me a little stool to stand on. Their breath was awful, because most of them were boozers. I got two shillings a week and it was a lot of hours.

Mr David Cooper

Miss Broadhurst's bakery

I was fourteen in 1934 and I left school. I went to work in a bake-house just at the bottom of Pickford Lane; it's still a confectioner's now, after all this time. It was owned by Miss Broadhurst, who opened the shop. While I was there, she did marry, and became Mrs Sam Higginbottom. In those days, if you were a baker and confectioner, you did it all. You baked your bread, you did your tea-cakes (plain, brown, currant, whatever); we used to do meat pies, large and small, and potato pies. Then we'd go on to the fancies. There was sandwiches, madeira cake, buns, flat cream buns, chocolate boxes, raspberry buns, every different kind of confectionery. The bake-house was hot, but we'd open the door and the windows.

Mrs Alice Edwards

Factory girl

I loved sewing when I was at school, and, when I left, me mum wanted me to be a tailoress. I started work with an elderly – well, I thought she was old – lady, but it was horrible, sewing by hand, buttonholes, very slow. I didn't want that; I wanted to be with other girls. I went to work as a machinist in a factory. We had the wireless going and we used to sing all day. Every morning we used to have 'Workers' Playtime,' because it was during the war. We had air-raid shelters, but we never went in them, even when the sirens went. I worked there till I was eighteen and then I moved to another clothing factory in Ashton. I've sewn everything there is to sew, from christening robes to body bags.

Mrs Joyce Hall

Girls from the weaving shed at Leach's Mill, Stalybridge, 1927. May Goddard (Mrs May Redford) is on the extreme left of the front row.

Office junior

My first job was as office junior at Thompson and Cooke, Solicitors, in Stalybridge. I did everything, everything wrong. Of course, they sent me to the post office for some red tape, and I went. One day a man came in with a parcel. He just said, 'For Mr Cooke'. 'What name is it, please?' 'Charlie.' I didn't look at the parcel. I took it up and gave it to Mr Cooke and said, 'Charlie's left this for you.' 'I think you mean Mr Chorley,' he said. I had to do the switchboard, the up and down pegs they had in those days. I soon learned that and enjoyed it. One day I announced to Mr Hamer, 'The District Bank are on the phone, about Mrs Olive Hall, deceased.' 'Deceased, Jean?' he said. 'That's my living mother-in-law.' One day they sent me down Manchester to the Midland Hotel with some papers that had been forgotten. I thought I was the bee's knees, going to the Midland Hotel.

Mrs Jean Pilling

Miss Larner's hat shop

When I left school at fourteen, in the 1930s, I went to work in a hat shop on Market Street, Stalybridge. The lady who owned it was called Miss Larner. I had to light the fire in the morning when I went upstairs. She wouldn't buy firewood; I had to light it with cardboard. If it didn't get going, oh dear! I didn't get the cane, but it was bad enough, her shouting at me. I had to fold the cardboard up and stick it in the grate and hope it would catch light. She never married and she used to keep open on Saturday night until eight o'clock. They could keep open as long as they wanted then. I would be up there doing her hat boxes for her, and all for 5s a week.

Mrs Lily Gover

Ruling by the book

I left Lakes Road school when I was fourteen in 1932 and I went to work at a printer and bookbinder in Hyde; it was called Cartwright and Rattrey. It was a family business. I worked in the ruling department there. They made exercise books and also used to do bus guides, small North Western bus guides. I used to sit at a machine feeding sheets of paper in and the machine ruled lines on it. I didn't like the job very much, but I stayed till I was twenty-one.

Mrs Evelyn Whitworth

Running to work

I worked at an engineering place called Ferguson and Palin in Openshaw. I used to have to run to work. I had to catch the first bus out of the SHMD depot at Stalybridge to Ashton. Dad used to get me up. He used to say, 'C'mon now, time to get up.' He'd be out first and I'd be after him. The first bus out of the depot would be coming along Tame Valley on its way to Ashton. I used to get off at the terminus in St Michael's Square and I'd have to run all the way along Stamford Street to the Wine Lodge, to catch me bus for Openshaw at five to seven.

Mrs Betty Jones

Three girls at the gas works

I went to work in the mill when I left school, but one mill after another kept closing down. There were a gas works then, up Acres Lane. I got a job there. There were three of us girls, me, Ada Clark and Edie Norton. We were painting gasometers and painting inside in winter. The gasometers were low down when we started. The manager were called Mr Restall.

Mrs Edith Jones

Stalybridge Millbrook group of National Fire Service.

Price's cake shop

I left school at the end of the 1940s. There were this cake shop on Market Street, Stalybridge – Price's. If they had any bread left at night they used to give it to my dad to feed the animals. I always wanted to work in that cake shop. The lady there said she'd ask the management if they wanted somebody, 'cos one of the ladies was finishing. I had to go for an interview to Clayton in Manchester, with a Mr Wilson, and I got the job. I worked nine till six o'clock, and had a half-day off on Tuesdays.

On a Monday morning, before everything was delivered from a big bake-house in Clayton, you had to wipe everything down, all the shop walls, the ceiling and everything. When the shop shut, you had to mop all the floors. I earned about £4 12s a week. The manageress of the shop was called Miss Tobin. She was a Catholic and she always went to church, to mass. In the morning I always had to sweep outside the shop to the gutter and pick all the litter up. There was another girl who worked with me there. She had asthma. When you went to the toilet, you had to go down into the cellar. Coal was kept down there and, when you went down to the toilet, you had to bring a shovel of coal up for the fire. This poor girl could hardly get her breath, so I'd say, 'When you go to the toilet, leave a shovel of coal at bottom of stairs and I'll go for it.' The toilets were out in the yard and the river were running past. If it rained the river were very high and you'd think, 'Cripes, if the toilet goes, I'll go with it!'

Mrs Margaret Green

A week is a long time

My father's parents lived on Pickford Lane. My grandfather was a skip-maker, a basket-maker, if you like. Cops are small tubes of cotton and they were packed in these big skips. The skip would be about four or five feet square and the same depth. My grand-

87

Millbrook Wesleyans in the garden of Mr and Mrs Lowe, mill-owners, c. 1914.

father's job was to make and repair these skips. He was employed by a firm of skip-makers at Guide Bridge. They sent him out working at a mill for a week. He went to the Clarence Mill, down Sandy Lane here in Dukinfield. He was sent here for a week; he was there for forty-three years. He had to go, every Friday tea time, down Guide Bridge for his wages. They didn't send them up.

Mr Fred Travis

Nightdresses – 1s 11d a dozen

When I was twenty one a friend of my mother, who had a pawn shop, and who knew a lot of Manchester businessmen, took me down to Manchester, because I was out of a job. I started work there, sewing, and I made a dozen night dresses a day and got 1s 11d for that. I stayed there until they opened a place in Cheetham's Mill here – Lister's – and then three of us come from Manchester and started there. I worked there for forty-five years.

Mrs May Redford

Pa, put your apron on!

My grandparents had a baker's shop on St George's Street. I remember my granddad taking the loaves out of the oven at the back and giving them to my brother and myself – red hot – to run through to the lobby and put them on the table to cool. My granddad, long-suffering, poor thing! – he used to wear a hessian apron for the oven work. Sometimes he'd come through to the shop to serve. He had to put a white apron over the top of the hessian one. If he ever dared to go into the shop without the white apron, I can hear my grandma now. She'd come to the door and shout, 'Pa, you haven't got your apron on. Come and get it!' All this in front of the customers. He was only a little bloke and he'd toddle off.

Mrs Joyce Travis

Seeking work in the Depression

My father were out of work for five years during the Depression, 1926 to 1931. I left school in 1929. I wanted to be a butcher; I were promised a job as a butcher but it never materialized. Then I went round the joiners' shops and nobody wanted any. They said they didn't want lads when there were trained men stood at the gates every morning, waiting for jobs. Kay Street Mission, Cockbrook Mission

Hall, that's where the unemployment offices were. My grandfather, he finished when he were sixty-three; he had to go and sign on and it practically broke his heart. My father, one time, he went to the unemployment place and they told him there were no dole for him. When he asked why not, they said, 'Your children are earning enough to keep you.' He came back and my mother said he broke his heart. 'To think I've come to having my children to keep me,' he said.

Mr Percy Norton

Apprentice at the cooperage

When I left school at fifteen in the early 1950s, I became an apprentice at a cooperage. When an apprentice came out of his time, he had to make his own barrel and then get rolled around the yard in it, and have mud thrown over him; then there's a great party afterwards. I served my apprenticeship at the cooperage, making beer barrels. After that I went to

Coming-out ceremony at Buckley's Cooperage, Tame Valley.

Coming-out ceremony at Buckley's Cooperage, Tame Valley.

Greengate Wood-Turning, another firm on Tame Valley. They made spindles, but the main thing they made was kitchen-tool handles for Prestige. They would turn out 25 million kitchen-tool handles a year, working a day and night shift.

Mr John Perry

The grocer's boy

I left school at fourteen, at the time of the Depression. My father and my elder brother were unemployed, but my elder sister were working. My younger brother won a scholarship to go to Hyde Grammar school, but they had to take him away early because they couldn't afford to keep him going there. I did get a job, as a grocer's boy, with Ernie Cope, a grocer in Dukinfield. His shop was on the corner of Peel Street. I got the marvellous sum of 7s a week. That was from nine o'clock in the morning until six o'clock in the evening

six days a week. Tuesday was early closing. My father was out of work and looking for a job all round the district. I used to go with him. We walked for miles. As a grocer's boy I did delivering orders. I used to do a great amount of carrying – sacks of sugar, sacks of flour, carried them on me back into the shop. Did sweeping up and cleaning. I remember two jobs in particular. The bacon used to be on view in the window, rows of bacon on shelves. Summertime it used to get flyblown. The following day you'd see the maggots. My job was to take the bacon into the back, to tubs of boiling water, which brought the maggots out; give it a wipe and a polish, then back on the shelves again! The flour used to be in 140lb bags. We'd notice a tiny hole in the bottom one morning; a mouse had been in. My job was to sieve all of that bag full of flour for mouse droppings. I might not come across any, but all the bag had to be sieved and put into another bag. The flour, sugar, tea, coffee, rice, currants were all made up into little bags and weighed – by me. We always had a cat to keep mice down. Of course, cats are always having kittens. The fellow in the shop used to make me drown those kittens.

Mr Fred Travis

The egg-butty boy

When I was delivering papers for Miss Sidebottom, I had to go to Moorhouse's Brass Finishing shop. I had three papers to deliver in the foundry, about five in another part and six upstairs. The lad who showed me the route was starting work and that's how I got his round. First day I was on my own, I come in and put this paper on a bench. It was about 7.55 a.m. then and they were still working. I finished off in top room and then I went home. Next day, when I went in, I threw paper on his bench and were walking away. 'Hey, where were you yesterday?' I thought he'd lost his paper and I said, 'I put your paper on the bench, mister.' He said, 'I'm not talking about that. Where were you yesterday?' 'Well,' I said, 'when I'd delivered around the shop, I went home.' 'Yes,' he said, 'and next time you do that, I'll box your ears. You don't go out of here until you've had an egg butty off me.' Every morning after that, without fail, he gave me an egg butty.

Mr Alex Cox

'Mother! I've got a job!'

I was stood watching them slaughtering the animals one morning when a chap came along with a barrow. He were picking tripes up. I didn't know what they were. He said to me, 'Do you want a job? Well, there's a chap called Tom Brown and he wants a lad for doing tripe.' 'Where is it?' I said. 'It's back Castle Street.' I knew where that was and off I went; I ran like hell. I got there and I said, 'I believe you want a lad.' He said, 'Have you got your leaving papers?' 'Not on me.' 'Well, you can start in the morning. Come at seven o'clock.' I run home. My mother were mopping bedrooms. I run upstairs, two at a time. 'Mother! Mother!' I shouted, 'I've got a job!' It was her birthday and she said it were the best birthday she'd ever had.

Mr Percy Norton

The last tripe-dresser

I worked in the tripe-dressing trade all my working life, from time I were fourteen. The tripe is the stomach of a cow. We went to the slaughterhouse and fetched it back. Then you cut the stomach open and washed it to get all the grass out; then you had to scald it. You put half a can of soda in, then you throw all the stomachs in, and you put two buckets of boiling water to one of cold. When they'd been in about half an hour, you just warmed it all up until the lining of the stomach came off and it were white underneath, though, if they'd been eating a lot of grass, it were still green. Then you boiled it. One fellow said to me, 'How long do you boil it?' I said, 'Until it's done,' and he said, 'Any fool knows that,' and he give me a right smack on the ear for me pains. You had to feel at the tripes and if your thumbnail went through you knew it were done. Then you cooled it down, and you got peroxide of hydrogen and bleached it. You had to take the skin off the back then. That was tripe dressing. The shop went in the name of Hutchison and Strachan. Jim Hutchison died when I were nineteen and I carried the business on myself then, though Strachan, who was a grocer, was still a partner in it. I were still there in 1958 when the council put a compulsory purchase order on it and we had to close. The shop had been at the back of Castle Street, Stalybridge.

Mr Percy Norton

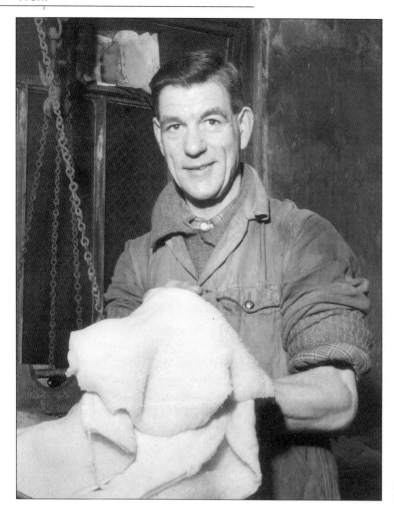

Percy Norton, the last tripe-dresser in Stalybridge.

The projectionist's lot

When I left school during the war I got a job in an accountant's office in Manchester, but I didn't like it. My dad got me a job as a projectionist at the Pavilion Cinema in Ashton, and I loved it. I was there till I joined up when I was eighteen. The first film I showed was *One of Our Aircraft is Missing* and second was *They Died With Their Boots On*, with Errol Flynn. They weren't good hours; you'd go in at ten o'clock in the morning, till twelve o'clock say, and clean up and get things ready; then we'd be in at 2.00 p.m. for a 2.30 p.m. start to the afternoon performance; then there were two shows at night. It was ten o'clock at night when you were over. Then I had to come home in the blackout, or do firewatch when I turned sixteen. But the cinema trade was quickly absorbed into you – 'The show must go on'. On 4 November 1944 we were showing a film called *Forever and a Day*; it had a galaxy of stars. Ray Milland came through a door and next to him was Anna Neagle. At that particular point there was a flash and the film went up in flames; we lost 2,000 feet of film. The flames overcame me, because I was on the inside of the projector, the wrong side of the flames. I came behind the machines and the chief projectionist – I was only the assistant – was squirting the fire extinguisher where he knew I had to come through. It was ten to nine at night. We cleared the building and, of course, immediately started cleaning up. The projector, the cog-wheels and everything was actually fused with the heat. We were told to come back for eight o'clock in the morning. We had new projector heads and new sound equipment and the show opened the following day, 5 November at 2.30 p.m. I got 10s bonus for that. The manager at the time was Stanley Britland. At that time the Pavilion and the Odeon at Guide Bridge sometimes showed the same film. There was great co-operation between us and the Odeon for us to keep showing the film. We synchronised the showings and, when a reel came off at the Odeon, it was put into a taxi and whipped straight up to the Pavilion, in time for us to show it. We had to do that every showing, three times a day.

Mr Tom Evans

'Not everybody can do this'

My grandad used to work in a cellar because that was where all the cops were kept, to keep them damp, so the thread wouldn't break. I remember seeing him down in the cellars. He used to have a board, about eight-feet square, that he worked on. He always sat down with his back to the wall, on a folded sack, with his legs crossed and the skip in front. There was a spike in this board and they stuck the basket on it; as he was weaving, he kept turning the basket round. He used to say, and he wasn't being facetious at all, 'Thou knows, not everybody can do this; they canna stand sitting down.'

Mr Fred Travis

'I'm not an office person!'

When I left school, I needed a job. You had to go to the Labour Exchange. They gave you a little green card. There was none of this roaming the streets. Your mum used to frog-march you to the Labour Exchange. I was supposed to go to a firm called Waterlow's, to learn bookbinding; but that just fell through. They said, 'Well, you can have this job at Daniel Adamson's in the office.' I thought, 'I'm not an office person at all.' My mum took me and we went in one of the offices and there were two directors. They interviewed me and I got the job. I was office girl for three years, which I thoroughly enjoyed.

Mrs Pat Bolt

6 Two World Wars

1914-1918

Marching off to war

I was four years old when the First World War started in 1914. I can remember the Territorials marching in the First World War, y'know. They used to have a drill hall in Stalybridge and they marched down from the drill hall. We were stood at the corner of Rose Terrace and we watched them go past. They were going off to war. I often wonder how many of them came back. They were all only quite young.

Mrs Nellie Howarth

The peace parade

I remember queuing up for food in the First World War; they didn't have rationing, like they had in the Second World War; it was a good thing, rationing. I can remember queuing up for certain things during the First World War. There wasn't a blackout, like in the 1939-1945 war. I can remember the peace parade after the First World War; it was a big parade and all the schools and that joined in. As regards the actual warfare, I don't remember a lot – only that we had friends who went to the war, of course.

Mrs Nellie Howarth

Memories of the First World War

In 1914, when the war started, I was nine. Somebody come in our house and said to my mum, 'Hey, Harry's enlisted!' My mother said, 'Well, if he thinks more about his King and country than he does about his wife and family, let him go.' My dad and my eldest brother were in the army during the First World War. My mother had a good time when my father were in th'army. She could go to the pictures with my auntie. My father were only in the army about nine months, but he won the war; he thought he did anyway. I remember Zeppelins coming over.

Mrs Alice Young

The Scotch plaid bonnet

I was just eight when the First World War ended. I remember we had to go and queue up for things. Where the Co-op is there was a row of shops and in them was Barlow's; they had a beef shop and a pork shop. I used to go to Barlow's and queue up until mother came. She'd do other things at home and then, when it came time for shopping, she'd come down and take my place in the queue. She used to give me a ha'penny and I'd go in the coffee shop next door for a ha'penny cup of coffee. She always made my clothes and she made me a fur bonnet with Scotch plaid strings. I hated that bonnet. I can't remember what the coat were like, but I can remember that bonnet. It were awful. I always went for my ha'penny cup of coffee, then I went home and waited till she'd got served and she'd come back and get me ready for school.

Mrs May Redford

'Sort your own out!'

My mother's father was a sergeant major in the First World War. When he came home after the war, he came back to his wife and five children. My mother tells the story that one day my grandma was putting the dinner out. One said, 'I don't want any of that.' Another said, 'Can I have a bit more of that?' He said, 'Sort your own out', and he upended the table; my grandma had just cleaned all the kitchen floor. So, he seems to have been rather intolerant when he came out of the army. I don't suppose the children ever did that again. He was a tall, handsome fellow, and my grandma was small, plumpish, really bonny. They were a good-looking couple.

Mrs Joyce Travis

1939-1945

Time off!

While the war was on, if you got an air raid during the night, you didn't go into school while ten o'clock the next morning; you got an hour off. If the air raid was really bad and went on till the early morning, you didn't have to go in while dinnertime. Then you only had the afternoon in school, which suited me fine, because I didn't like school.

Mr Bob Sleigh

Shelter at Roberts' farm

At the back of the houses on Lodge Lane, down at the bottom, was a little farm, Roberts' Farm. It was just a little smallholding really, with a bit of ground, but they always called it Roberts' Farm. We didn't have any air-raid shelters at the back of the houses so we all used to go down to Roberts' Farm when the siren went. We used to go in the shippons there and sing. We had gas masks. My brother had a red one, a Mickey Mouse one, because he wasn't old enough for a proper one; we used to have these boxes to put them in. My father was in the Fire Brigade Reserve; he used to stand at t' window with his tin helmet and his axe. Sometimes my mother used to turn the settee upside down and we'd go under there during an air-raid warning, or she'd put my brother in a tub under the stairs.

Mrs Pat Bolt

Swapping shrapnel lumps

I was brought up in wartime. It must have been a frightening time to my parents, but to me war was a wonderful experience, a time of great excitement. I'd lie in bed at night in Stalybridge and the German bombers used to come right over Stalybridge to fly down to Manchester. There was an anti-aircraft site where the Brushes reservoirs are now; you'd hear the guns going off at night. You'd hear shrapnel rattling across the roofs. Obviously it would be from the guns, but to us lads it was from foreign aircraft, bits of Germany dropping on us. At morning there were always a mad scurry to get up first and find the best lumps of shrapnel. We used to go and gather this stuff. There were bits of exploded shells. It was dangerous stuff; it had edges like razors. We'd gather this stuff in bags and then we'd

Stalybridge Home Guard 1942-43.

swap it. I had three uncles who fought in the war and they'd all bring souvenirs back – foreign coins, bits of German uniform, stripes and badges. We'd collect all this and swap it. The whole of the country was like a big car-boot sale, everybody swapping stuff. I had a badge off an SS car; it was all enamelled and it was the pride and joy of my collection. SS daggers would come back, even a couple of guns, a Luger, a Mauser, a couple of British guns which somebody's father had brought back and he'd nicked out of the house to show us. Oh yes, the war was a time of great excitement, if you were a lad!

Mr Ron Watkins

Falling shrapnel

The war wasn't that fearsome for us. I do remember my brother coming home on leave. He had take out a girl I worked with who lived down Clayton, and I'd gone with them.

I can remember walking home from Clayton with my brother and somebody else, and there was stuff dropping. It must have been shrapnel. It was dropping all round us. I tell you, ignorance is bliss; we could have been killed, couldn't we?

Mrs Joyce Travis

Finding the way in the blackout

I lived in Astley Street during the war; we had a small house there. I remember the blackout. I used to go to my mother's a lot; she and my father still lived in George Street then, and she wasn't always well. I used to walk in the blackout, backward and forward, with the pram with the two children. My husband was a very handy man. He made a light what said 'PRAM' in a box, and cut it out and put it on the front; there was a battery and switch inside the pram. In the blackout I switched that on

Dukinfield Home Guard marching past the town hall. Chapel Street is in the background.

and people could see I were coming. We had gas masks, and we had one for the babies, but I don't think we ever used them. I remember the rationing. You had to manage, didn't you? I had an auntie who lived in Wales. She had fruit trees and kept chickens, so she used to visit and bring eggs and stuff for us.

Mrs Evelyn Whitworth

Box making and barrage balloons

I went from school to learn fancy box-making at Peter Blythe's in Audenshaw, and I stayed there four or five years until war broke out. Then I went to work at Kenyon's here in Dukinfield, on Railway Street. We were doing balloon rigging, making the rigging for barrage balloons. Later I went to a factory that they opened on Globe Lane, where the wagon works used to be. During the war it was split into two parts. There was a part at the top called Stone's and the other half was Dukinfield factory. They used to bring all these shells that had been used – shell cases that had been fired. You used to have to put them through big washing machines and clean them; then they would have the dents knocked out of them and be redone so that they could be fired again. They made shell cases too. It was hard work.

Mrs Nellie Preston

Mickey Mouse gas masks

The house where we lived had a cellar, which was always warm. We made a bed down there and we used to go down when the air raids were on. My niece lived up Kay Street and, when the sirens went, she used to leave her mother there and run down to come in our cellar. We used to stop in there till the all clear went. We had a big gas mask for our Philip; it

was shaped like a Mickey Mouse, but we never used it. I remember once I were going on Heyrod Road and a policeman stopped me for me identity card. I thought it were awful. 'I've always lived in Stalybridge,' I said. 'Well,' he said, 'it doesn't matter. I have to look at it.'

Mrs May Redford

Uneasy on the market ground

Every night you could hear planes going over. We always had the idea that a lot of them were going over to Liverpool. You could have set your clock at the time those planes went over. One night we'd been out, a Sunday night – I don't know if it were the night Manchester got the Blitz. We were with some friends. They lived high up; we stood at their bedroom window and watched the bombers ring Manchester with a ring of fire. They wanted us to stay the night, but we came home, because my mother was on her own. We were crossing the market ground and it's the only time I felt uneasy. You could hear the shrapnel, but you couldn't see it. We were really glad when we got off the market ground. It wasn't the planes; it was the guns.

Mrs Nellie Howarth

The doodlebug

I don't remember a lot about the war, but I do remember, one night, a doodlebug coming over. We were gone to bed one night and there was this here noise. Mum said, 'Doodle-bug.' We used to go downstairs; we had a pantry that went under [the kitchen] a bit, so we used to go down there. Otherwise we'd have had to go in the shelter which was higher up Tame Valley. Mum said, 'We'll go down in the pantry; happen it'll go over.'

Mrs Betty Jones

NEW PRINCE'S-STALYBRIDGE

MATINEES: Monday, Tuesday, Thursday, Saturday at 2-15 p.m.   Tel. 2485.
EVENINGS: CONTINUOUS from 6 p.m. (Saturday included).

OCTOBER 6th WEEK—Monday and Tuesday, TWO DAYS ONLY:

SIDNEY TOLER in	JEAN ROGERS and ROBERT STERLING in—
MURDER OVER NEW YORK	**YESTERDAY'S HEROES**

Wednesday, Thursday, Friday and Saturday—FOUR DAYS ONLY:

The glory of the world's greatest romance lives again

LOUIS HAYWARD, JOAN BENNETT and GEORGE SANDERS in

The SON of MONTE CRISTO

PLEASE CARRY YOUR GAS-MASK.

Advertisement for the New Princess Cinema, October 1941. Notice the exhortation at the bottom, 'Please carry your gas mask.'

A teenager's memories of the Second World War

The war didn't really touch Stalybridge very much. I saw a doodlebug once, early morning, going over Mottram Road, when I was going to work. There was an odd bomb fell in Stalybridge, but nobody was hurt. I knew about mothers and fathers losing their sons, and girls I worked with whose boyfriends had been killed. I remember the morning when it was the invasion and planes, hundreds and hundreds of planes, went over. We lived up there, Brushes Estate, and it was a clear morning. We used to go to the pictures a lot and, when they'd say, 'There's an air raid on,' you used to have to all come out and go to the shelter. An odd Saturday we'd have what they called a 'Wings for Victory' parade. Each town tried to buy a part of a Spitfire. You saved up your sixpences and stuck a stamp on a card. After so much was raised this little arrow used to go up outside the town hall. We probably bought a wheel for a Spitfire or something. I did follow the war closely in the newspapers; although I were only a young girl, I were very interested. I still have my identity card. We used to have a little identity chain around our neck, with our identity number on. Gas masks? Yes. They used to test them. They put a little bit of blotting paper underneath and we had to breathe in; then they'd look and, if there were any little holes, you had to go to Market Street and get another one. But we never used them. I can remember going into the air-raid shelters when I was young at Stalybridge

Central school. We used to have little 'iron rations' to eat, if we were in a long time. We were never in a long time, but I used to eat them just the same.

Mrs Joyce Hall

A Dukinfield boy's memories

I was at the Moravian school when the war started. They shut the schools because they expected to be bombed straight away. We had a month or two months' holiday before they decided we'd have to go to school. I remember I was stood on the steps there, looking over Ashton, when the news came through that France had fallen. It said, 'We're alone now.' The Germans had taken over nearly all Europe; there was only us left. I remember going to school when the doodle-bugs, flying bombs, were going over. I were walking across the town hall when I saw one going over; it landed in Oldham. During the war you had a week's holiday; the only places you could go were Blackpool, Southport or Llandudno. My auntie took me on train to Southport to try to find digs for the holiday. The train back from Southport took about four hours to get to Manchester. It kept getting pushed in sidings with the raids on. We had to walk from Manchester to my auntie's son's house in Audenshaw, while bombs were dropping and guns were firing.

Mr Kenneth Gee

Life during the war

Les got his call-up papers on his twenty-first birthday – 18 January 1940 – and he went in the army. We got married before he went abroad at Wellington Street Methodist. We didn't have a big do; I had a costume and a spray and I made my wedding cake because I was a baker. Things were on ration, but we managed. The cake wasn't iced all over. We put a ribbon round it and just iced the top and piped over the ribbon. Trifle was a luxury. We did our own catering. And we had the reception at home. We used to get one egg a week on rationing. When he was due for a leave, I used to save my egg for him. I used to have dried egg and my mother wasn't very happy about it. We used to write every day. The soldiers, when they wrote, weren't allowed to say where they were. They were only allowed one letter for two people. A friend who shared with Les, Bert Kilner, lived at Denbydale. His wife was a nursing auxiliary. They got this one airmail; Bert would write one page, Les another. It could only go to one address, so it went to Bert's; his wife tore off what was hers and sent the other part to me. Letters were censored. They didn't cross it out; they cut it out. Les and Bert weren't able to tell us where they were, but they said if you noticed the letters on her apron – NA for Nursing Auxiliary – you'd know where they were – North Africa.

Mrs Alice Edwards

Seeing stars

During the war we lived at 12 Astley Street, Castle Hall; Drill Hall were at the end of the street. I remember being in my brother's; he used to live in a little street called Ogden Street. On a Sunday night we used to go round to each other's houses, playing cards and having supper. It was a Sunday and Christmas Eve was on the Tuesday. We kept coming out and looking at Manchester and it were all ablaze. We set off home, and there was much banging and crashing. We got home and went to bed. Next news I could see the stars through the roof. A bomb, a delayed-action bomb, had come through the ceiling. I remember looking at the clock and it were ten-past two. I also remember coughing in the fumes and the plaster. We'd not heard anything. I said, 'Oh, Len, there's summat wrong somewhere.' Everything were white like when you go in a furniture shop and everything's covered up. When he got up and stepped in it, it came up in a cloud and made you cough more. He wakened up and I said, 'Ooh, look! You can see stars!' Absolutely gormless. We went to the top of the stairs. We had some ornaments and I kicked one and it went bom, bom, bom down the stairs. We kept them downstairs in the kitchen, so they must have been blown upstairs. Len looked through window and said, 'Summat's dropped somewhere.' I remember getting dressed and he said, 'We'd better go out; we don't know what's going on.' He got out; it were blackout and we couldn't light up. He just jumped over the hole. I went down in it. He says, 'Where are you?' I says, 'I'm here.' He come down cellar as far as he could. That was a shock, tumbling down the hole where the bomb was. It took part of the bed and there was a clean hole in the carpet, a clean hole in the lounge and it took part of the settee. I must have screamed, because our neighbour, Jimmy Lawton, heard me and said 'Come on in my house.' They didn't come for eight weeks to take the bomb away; we had to go down to Len's mother's and live there. When Jimmy Lawton took us to his house, his mother-in-law were up. She said, 'They're a couple getting on, aren't they?' Our hair was grey from the dust. The bomb had buried itself in the cellar; it had a concrete floor and the bomb had buried itself in the soil underneath. The date was on the bomb.

Mrs Edith Jones

The burglars

When we come back to the house, after the damage was repaired, we had burglars. Len were fire-watching in Cheetham's Park. He used to go one or two nights a week. I were in bed. We had burglars. They took all me clothing coupons, what little bit of money we had, and the ration books. When Len came home, the door were wide open and I were asleep in bed.

Mrs Edith Jones

Girls in the army

I was called up in 1942, when I was twenty-one. We could go in the army, the air force or industry. I didn't want to go into industry, so I chose the army; best thing I ever did in my life. First of all I went to Lancaster for three weeks' training. We trained at Ripley Hall, which had been a monastery and is now a boys' school. We did square bashing; never did any again. From there we went to Wilton; we stayed in what is supposed to be one of the country's poshest houses and it was the most miserable night of our lives. The girl who opened the door to us said, 'The officer's not here.' I said, 'We'll have to wait. We've come down from Lancaster. Can't we have a meal?' We'd had sardine sandwiches given to us at Lancaster and we'd had nothing since. She said, 'There's nothing cooked, but I'll find you something.' What did she bring us? Sardine sandwiches. The officer came back and said, 'I don't know why they've sent you here. I don't need anybody.' She found us beds. Years later, when my friend and I were both married, I said to her, 'I cried myself to sleep that night at Wilton.' She said, 'I didn't know you were crying. I was as well.' We were absolutely miserable. Next morning they took us down to Salisbury, to Southern Command HQ. They gave us rooms on the first floor – great big embrasure windows that had chintz cushions in; sheets, settees, Indian carpets, a big fire (it was October) and we looked out over our own little garden. Just across the street there was a low wall, and there beyond was Salisbury Cathedral –

beautiful! We used to have to stay in on Thursday nights. One of the girls, Wendy from Bournemouth, said, 'I hate Thursday night. I hate having to stay in.' 'Wendy,' I said, 'if you came North, Thursday nights would have been spent black-leading, washing the lino and stoning the kitchen floor.' 'What's black-leading?' she asked.

Mrs Ethel Anderson

Pigs can fly

I suppose, right from war breaking out, as children we didn't know there was a war on. We didn't get the enormity of it. I remember on a Friday night, as war was declared on the Sunday, we were playing out in the fields and, as we were coming home, it was still daylight, and over Manchester we could see what looked like a lot of flying pigs. We didn't know what they were, but they were barrage balloons. There was a huge amount of them, all over Manchester. Our gas masks were very handy for carrying things about in. We soon stopped carrying them about everywhere. It was knocked into us at first, 'You take these everywhere you go.' But people slowly got apathetic. We had to take them to school. We always had to have a block of chocolate in them, as emergency rations.

Mr Tom Evans

The British Restaurant

We had a British Restaurant in Stalybridge, where Rothwell's furniture shop used to be. Originally it was what they called a coffee tavern. Then it became the British

Ethel Downs (Anderson) in her army uniform in Bishop's Palace Garden, Salisbury Cathedral, 18 April 1943.

Stalybridge Whit Walks on Trinity Street in the 1950s. The building on the right housed the British Restaurant during the war.

Restaurant. Then, when that closed, a man named Rothwell took it over as a furniture store.

Mrs Nellie Howarth

Where's the hospital?

Three of us were going down to London as shelter nurses. They sent a telegram to say we were to transfer to the military hospital at Halsey in Bedfordshire. Nobody knew where it was; we asked at the station and they told us to get a train to Peterborough and ask again when we got there. We started off early morning and it was ten at night when we got to this place. It was just a country village; there wasn't even a proper station, just a platform. It was pitch black; they put us off

the train and we had no idea where to go. Eventually we found some cottages and knocked them up. This lady came out and she told us to walk along this road till we came to the big gates. Of course, there were sentries at these gates. They put our suitcases in the guardroom, and they took us up to the hospital, which was two miles from the gates. When we got there and reported, she said, 'Where's your luggage?' We said, 'In the garden.' Bet she thought, 'Oh, a bit simple.'

Miss Annice Ritson

Recommended for mechanic

When I went in the army, they sent us to the Middle East. We went up the desert in what they called 'job-columns,' which were suicide

Street party on Elgin Street to celebrate the end of the Second World War.

squads, nothing else. First action I was in, they all got killed on the gun. I were the only one left standing. I picked the gun up and I had twenty-six blokes at the back of me. The officer said, 'I'll see you get recommended for an MM.' I thought, "I'm going to be made a motor mechanic.' I never thought about the Military Medal. I thought I were going to be made a motor mechanic because I had picked this gun up. In the event I got nothing; the officer got killed.

Mr Percy Norton

Johnny the evacuee

We had an evacuee. The WVS (Women's Voluntary Service) brought a group of children to the end of our road, to see if anybody would have them. They were just stood there, like little sheep, and everybody was looking at them. I ran out and I said, 'Can we have one, mum?' My mum was a soft-hearted lady and she said we could. 'I'm having a girl,' I said, but we only had room for a boy, because he could sleep with my brother. We had a boy called Johnny; he was a little Cockney, a right little smart-alec. He was with us for three years. My mum had very bad arthritis and so she eventually said to him, 'Johnny, the bombs have stopped dropping in London long ago. I'm sorry, you'll have to go back. I've had you for three years now.' He didn't want to go, but my mum got money together and paid his fare, and a suitcase of new clothes, including his first long trousers. Saturday off he went. Monday night we heard a shout; he was back. He'd only been home a

Street party in 1945 to celebrate the end of the Second World War. Johnny the evacuee is the boy to the right of the lady with a hat who is sitting at the head of the table.

Stayley Mill Peace celebration.

weekend. His mum didn't want him; she wrote and asked me mum would she adopt him, but she couldn't, with three of her own. He was with us another three years. Then he went back and we never heard another word from him.

Mrs Joyce Hall

Peace at last

I was working at the Pavilion cinema when the war with Germany ended. We shut the film off and put a slide on the screen – 'Hostilities will cease at such and such a time today.' I wrote that slide to put on the screen and it was a thrill for an eighteen-year old lad, ready to join up. I wrote the slide and I knew that the German war was over.

Mr Tom Evans

Leslie and the forbidden rifle

My father was secretary of the Dukinfield branch of the League of Nations, which was pressing for disarmament. My brother Leslie wanted to go into the Army. We had already lost one brother to the Army and my father wouldn't have it. Leslie worked in the mill and at the age of seventeen was already doing well. Promotion in the mill was not easy though, and Leslie used to say, 'I'm not waiting the rest of my life for somebody to die so that I can have his job. I must be off.' He wanted to go in the Army but my dad wouldn't sign for him. He joined the Territorial Army and they issued him with a rifle. Father said, 'You're not bringing that rifle in this house. This is my house; you're not bringing that rifle in here.' So Leslie used to call at Uncle Albert's and leave his rifle there. That was illegal, but if there was anything illegal I think Uncle Albert enjoyed it. He'd look after the rifle for Leslie until he went on parade at the armoury on Old Street in Ashton. When Leslie came back at night he would hand the rifle over to Uncle Albert, who lived next door to us, and then he'd come in – with no rifle! The day Leslie was eighteen he was in the Army, and he never came out. He went up and up and up, and he was a Lieutenant-Colonel when he finished. He went all over the world. He'd never have done anything like that if he'd stayed in the spinning mill. When the Second World War was on he was in the Bahamas. He said, 'Our biggest problem was keeping cool'.

David Cooper

7 Shopping and Leisure

Shopping on High Street, Stalybridge, in the 1920s

There was a little confectioner's in Tame Street; they sold other bits as well. Then we had a corner shop at the end of Robinson Street, in older property. There were shops on High Street, just below St John's, but the majority of shops lay between Hollins Street and Stanley Square. From the Buck Inn down to Stanley Square we used to say we had every shop you could need. We even had an arts and crafts shop, a good one. The father and sister of Miss Gregory, who taught at Central school for Girls, ran this shop. There was a draper's and a milliner's; the post office was there; three newsagents – Smith's, Williams' and Wright's; four butchers – Wilfred Hodgson on the corner of Tame Street and High Street, the Co-op across the way, Dalton's and Murgatroyd's. There was a wet fish shop, Arthur Upton's, and a tripe shop, three greengrocers, an ironmonger's, the Co-op grocery and a baby-linen shop. Then when

Stalybridge Carnival in Grosvenor Street, 1935.

you got to Stanley Square, there was another baby-linen shop and Mr Ibbotson, the cobbler. That was High Street, but we never called it High Street. 'I'm just going up Front Street, an errand.' One of the baby-linen shops was called Phyllis.' Then there was 'Skinny Bertha's.' I'd go to Sunday school on Sunday morning and Sunday afternoon. Then my dad would take me up to Skinny Bertha's and buy me a quarter of Terry's Devon Chocolates and my mother a quarter of Santoy mixtures, great big fondants, some with nuts in, some with cherries. He'd buy himself a quarter of butterscotch. The shop belonged to Bertha Kinder and was on the left-hand side going down towards Stanley Square. And she did give skinny measures!

Mrs Ethel Anderson

King Street, Dukinfield, 1920s

There were shops on either side, all the way up to Ashton, along Cavendish Street; we always walked to Ashton. There were Cook's grocer's; he had two shops, Joe Cook. Next door to one of them was Timothy White's chemist. Cope's grocer's was opposite the town hall. I remember Percy Davies, the butcher; it was a big butcher's shop on the corner. Crossing over Astley Street there was another grocer's shop; then Cooks had their other shop going up Astley Street. There was the Maypole Dairy, opposite the Princess Cinema. Percy Ashton's fish shop were a bit lower down. There was a flower shop, a herbalist's and Underwood, the solicitor's. There was a tripe shop on Astley Street and a good one on King Street. Then there was Miss Pickering's toy shop, where the children used to go for their toys. Miss Pickering was an institution in Dukinfield. Everyone went with their pennies and halfpennies to Miss Pickering; she was a wonderful woman. There were four butchers' shops – Ashworth's,

Grimes', Hadfield's and Costello's; my granddad used to have me going to the butchers' shops. Mrs Marshall had a nice dress shop on King Street. The Co-op was on Astley Street; it had a drapery department and a place where they sold shoes and things.

Miss Annice Ritson
and Mrs Nellie Preston

The patience of Miss Pickering

There was a shop called Miss Pickering's; it was a toy shop. Everybody knew Miss Pickering's and people remember her even now. She used to have a lot of patience if you were buying anything, even if it were only for a penny. She'd tell you how it worked and everything. I remember going there, when I were a little girl, for a penny doll and a packet of patchworks to make clothes for it.

Mrs Evelyn Whitworth

Lovely hot-cross buns

Years ago no shops opened on Sunday. You could go and knock on the back door and ask them for something and they'd probably let you have it, but they wouldn't open on Sunday. Sunday was a day of rest. When we lived up Back Vaudrey Street there was a nice confectioner's shop – Mrs Berman's. Their hot-cross buns were lovely. Nobody's ever made them like they did; they were lovely.

Mr Bob Sleigh
and Mrs Lily Gover

R.W. Booth and Mabel Radcliffe

Going towards Ashton, on the left-hand side, there were a few hardware shops. There was one shop that was my uncle's; he had a shoe-

King Street, Dukinfield.

shop and shoe-repairing business there, R.W. Booth. Across the way, facing that, George Street went up, where I used to live. There was a draper's shop at the bottom. She were called Mabel Radcliffe. She had clothes and underwear; always a big window full of clothes. She lived in a little house on the side, on George Street.

Mrs Evelyn Whitworth

Millbrook shops in the 1920s

There were plenty of shops in Millbrook. My mother used to go to Stalybridge with our Maggie, once a week, to the Maypole, because butter and sugar and everything else was cheaper there. But everything else were bought in Millbrook. There were grocers, greengrocers, butchers, a clothes shop, a

hairdresser's – Bagshaw's – Berry's, Sidebottom's fruit shop, Bradbury's chip shop, Turner's paper shop and the Co-op.

Mrs Alice Young

Victoria Road, Dukinfield, 1920s

When I was young, there was a confectioner's across the road from where I lived on Victoria Road. I used to look in the window at these lovely cakes, and I used to think, 'I'll buy those when I grow up.' The shop was called Beard's. There was another shop at the corner when I was very, very little; it was like a draper's shop and it was kept by two sisters called Barratt, Emilia and Jessie Barratt. It was stocked; you couldn't ask for the wrong thing in there; it was absolutely packed. Emilia was a great big woman. On the opposite corner to that was the Co-op. Those big crates that oranges used to get packed in, or onions, they used to be fastened up with rope, but not as we know it; this was hairy, prickly stuff. We used to go and ask for it for skipping ropes. Across the road there was a little house-windowed shop, a very busy grocer's shop; he was called Sidney Arnold. Then there was a very big-windowed chip shop called Cunningham's. We couldn't afford to buy chips. Just next to that was the war memorial. Then, at the next corner, next door to the Victoria pub, was Braithwaite's draper's shop. Then, just past a big mill, there was another shop called Goodwin's; she sold all sorts of things. Then there was Stelfox's off-license, which sold everything as well. Then, just at the corner, past Stelfox's, was a newsagent's called Dransfield's. On the other side, beyond Beard's, there was another big grocer's shop; then there was the little school and just past the school there was a butcher's shop.

Mrs Alice Edwards

Friday night shopping in Stalybridge, 1930s

When we lived in Knowl Street, my mum used to take us shopping every Friday night. If she had a little bit of money left over, we'd go and have a fish and chip supper in Melbourne Street. Then we used to go into Stalybridge market hall and she used to buy her green-grocery. If my father came with us, we used to go onto Market Street and buy an accu-mulator, if the wireless was starting to go wonky. We had to carry it careful, 'cos there was acid in. Sometimes, when they hadn't enough money for an accumulator, we were without wireless for a little while. Everything was excitement to us. Going shopping on Friday night was a great thing.

Mrs Joyce Hall

The top of Crescent Road in the late 1930s and early '40s

Going down Crescent Road there was Hoyle's, a DIY-hardware store; they sold lamp oil and buckets, all sorts of things; it was a really big shop and had hanging baskets outside. Mrs Clowes lived next door, then Mrs Roebuck. After that there were two or three shops. Bertharella's was next door; that's a name to conjure with. Bertharella's was a mixture of everything you could possibly want. My grandmother used to send me up there. I used to go and buy penny Oxos, and gas mantles were only a penny. She sold toys, skipping ropes, little dolls and things like that. But it was a horrible, smelly shop. She was the oldest lady I've ever seen in my life – very, very small, with big clothes and a shawl. Next door to Bertharella's was the sweet shop. I think the owner was called Percival. She always wore red, and always had powder and lipstick on. She was blonde. The shop sold everything in the sweet line: sugar mice, liquorice root – the kind of things you don't see nowadays.

Mrs Vera Win Hotchkiss

Tame Valley shopping, 1920s and '30s

We'd one fish and chip shop; I remember George Crossland being there. I think the Alston family may have had it before him. Then there was Rawson's confectioners. There was Spirit's shop, a sweet shop really; but they sold other things as well – hardware. It was a handy shop. They lived next door to us. Then there was another shop in what they called the New Row, as you came round the river. The row where I lived was Chadwick's Row, and there was a shop on the corner. It was called Bennett's and was a mixed business, groceries and greengrocery.

Mrs Betty Jones

A man for fair measure

Noah Rhodes had a sweet shop on the corner opposite 19 Row in Tame Valley in the Forties. It was just after the war and toffees were scarce. To make two ounces up, or whatever you had coupons for, he would cut a sweet in half. I've never seen that before or since. He cut sweets in half. You could think, 'What a fair man!' because he was making sure you got your two ounces or whatever. On the other hand, you might think, 'How mean! Couldn't he just have put a whole one on?'

Mrs Barbara Perry

Town Lane and Lodge Lane Co-op in the 1940s

We always had to have a white dress for the Whit Walks. We used to go to a shop called Mrs Howarth's, on Town Lane. I remember one year I had this lovely white dress and a bright red coat with a black collar. There was a lot of shops on Town Lane. There used to be a herbalist, Olivers', the two brothers. The library, of course, was on there, and a barber's shop. There was all sorts. At the end of Lodge Lane, where it joins Cheetham Hill Road, was the Co-op. It was a big Co-op. It had the trap doors at the top, and they used to take all the potatoes up in sacks. I could watch from our front. The entrance was on Cheetham Hill Road. It had long counters, the old, great big, long counters. They used to weigh everything, and there were pats of butter ooh lovely!. There was a chip shop on Lodge Lane and further down there was an off-license.

Mrs Pat Bolt

Silent movies and talkies

I went to the Palace and the New Princes cinemas in Stalybridge when I was a kid. The Palace was just the same as it is now, a balcony and a pit. We used to go in the afternoons, penny rush. It were full of kids. They were silent films; writing were underneath. They had a drum for when guns were going off, and a piano were playing. The first picture at the New Princes, when it opened, was *All Quiet on the Western Front*, and it was a silent picture. The week after they had a talkie, because Al Jolson were singing 'Sonny Boy.' They had all the Ziegfeld Follies films in the 1930s and '40s. We went one Christmas Day and it were a coloured film and we'd never seen one before. The scenery was marvellous.

Mr Percy Norton

Moorhouse's effects machine

A man named Moorhouse lost a lot of money on the cinema. He bought the Oddfellows Hall in Stalybridge and turned it into a cinema. They put an upstairs in and it was really a posh place. He spent thousands of pounds on perfecting an effects machine for cinema. He got it going, and he put it in the Oddfellows Hall. Then Talkies came out. They had all the effects on the film. His machine was obsolete and he lost a lot of money. I remember the Oxford Cinema in Dukinfield being built. It was at the top of Sandy Lane. The land belonged to Farmer Reece; he kept about eight cows in a shippon there. Then a coal merchant called Pogson took it over, and he had it until it was bought for the building of the Oxford. The cinema was really nice. It was built down steep. Everybody could see. They built it level with the road, and the road sloped. I think it was 6d up front, 9d at the back and 1s in the circle.

Mr Alex Cox

```
TEL:
2485   NEW PRINCE'S, Stalybridge
```

MATINEES: Monday, Tuesday, Thursday, Saturday at 2-30 p.m.

TWO MAGNIFICENT PROGRAMMES!

MAY 31st WEEK—MONDAY and TUESDAY (TWO DAYS ONLY)—
An amazing picture which sets a new record for thrills and mystery!

LIONEL BARRYMORE, Maureen O'Sullivan, Frank Lawton in

THE DEVIL DOLL

It will keep you glued to your seat in fascinated attention!

Also A PATSY KELLY-THELMA TODD 2-REEL COMEDY and
BRITISH LION VARIETIES, No. 4.

WEDNESDAY, THURSDAY, FRIDAY, SATURDAY—FOUR DAYS ONLY:

A colossal production which has awe-inspiring drama, romance, hair-raising thrills,
indescribable spectacle and beautiful music welded into a stupendous whole!

CLARK GABLE, JEANETTE MACDONALD, SPENCER TRACY in

SAN FRANCISCO

Few scenes in the whole history of motion pictures have been done with more
realism than the magnificent earthquake climax.

IT WILL THRILL YOU!

ALL THE WEEK   IN RESPONSE TO INSISTENT PUBLIC DEMAND,

THE GAUMONT-BRITISH FILM OF

The Abbey Coronation Ceremony

AND AT GREAT EXPENSE,

MARVELLOUS CORONATION SCENES IN GLORIOUS TECHNICOLOR!

Including the Procession, The Crown Jewels, Royal Residences, Peers and Peeresses
specially posing in their wonderful Coronation Robes, and the glittering State
Coach in all its splendour.

A MAGNIFICENT TESTIMONY TO A SUPREME OCCASION!

Owing to great length of programme—Evening Performances will commence at 6-15
ALL THE WEEK.   Saturday at 6-15 and 8-45 p.m.

Advert for the New Prince's, Stalybridge, 1937.

Stalybridge cinemas

Stalybridge had the New Princes; we had booked seats there every Saturday night, me and my mother and my dad. If my mother was here she could tell you what rows and what numbers. It was in the circle at the right hand side. Then there was the Hippodrome; it's the one that was a theatre originally, where 'It's a long way to Tipperary' was written. We used to go there, me and my dad; he loved all the comics, Abbott and Costello, George Formby and Frank Randle, and they were usually at the Hippodrome. It wasn't as nice as the New Princes; they used to say, 'Cinema sprayed with June,' but I think it was sprayed with flea something. Any thrillers, I used to go with my mother, 'cos she always liked reading and seeing thrillers. I remember going to see a film with her, when I was a little girl, which frightened me to death. It was about this old couple who had a cottage on the moors and at the end they sank in a bog. I think it was called *The Night Has Eyes*. It gave me nightmares.

Advertisement for the Oxford cinema, Dukinfield, 1941.

When I watched it on TV a few years ago, I thought there was nothing to it. We all went from Castle Hall school to see Shirley Temple in the one where she lived with her grandfather in the mountains – *Heidi*, is it? The first picture I went to see when I was courting with my husband was a real cheerful picture to see on your first date – *Odette*, where she has her fingernails pulled off.

Mrs Jean Pilling

Saturday night at the New Princes

The New Princes was across the way from where the Methodist church is now. When I was courting, in the 1930s, my husband used to play cricket. I used to take my niece to watch him play every Saturday afternoon. When they had done we always went to his house for tea and then we went to the New Princes. We hadn't much money. You had to book your seat. We always booked them on the back row, because there was one seat further on than the others, and my niece always sat on this so that she could see. First we always went to a toffee shop along the street. I can see us now, looking in this window. 'What shall we have, Marjorie?' 'Well, we'll have – no we won't. We'll have –.' Then we had to wait while she picked what she wanted; then we bought a quarter of toffee and that were our Saturday night treat. I remember one Saturday night we were going to Chester on an evening trip – half a crown to Chester. She came down and she said, 'Where are you going?' I said, 'We're going to Chester.' She said, 'I've got tuppence half-penny. Can I come?' She came.

Mrs May Redford

A fire hazard!

The Oddfellows Hall was converted to a cinema, the New Princes. The first film they showed there was *Under the Greenwood Tree*. It was only a small place, but I always thought it was a fire hazard. You seemed to go up endless corridors and around; you could hear people coming out. There was only one way in and one way out. It would never have passed fire inspection today. They had some nice films

113

The Palace cinema, Stalybridge.

Hob Hill School. The Oddfellows Hall, later the New Princes cinema, is opposite.

```
GRAND THEATRE    ::    STALYBRIDGE
JULY 9th AND DURING THE WEEK.
SPECIAL ENGAGEMENT OF MISS CONNIE DESMOND,
IN SONGS, MONOLOGUE AND DANCES.

MONDAY, TUESDAY, AND WEDNESDAY—
MILTON SILLS in—
"SEA TIGER"
Also "FOUR-FOOTED RANGER," featuring The Dog, DYNAMITE.
"MELTING MILLIONS" - - - Episode 7.

THURSDAY, FRIDAY, AND SATURDAY—
FRANCIS X BUSHMAN in—
"13th JUROR"
"SNARL OF THE TIGER" - - - Episode 3.
```

Advertisement for the Grand Theatre, Stalybridge.

there and it was a cosy cinema. I also remember the Oxford cinema being built in Dukinfield. We used to go to childrens' matinées on Saturday afternoons at the Palace. The audience was all children. They used to have the serials that went on week after week – *Pearl White* and that.

Mrs Nellie Howarth

How many for the price of two?

One time I went along with some friends to the New Princes cinema, but money was a problem. To get in the stalls one paid at the box office, which was quite high, and then had to walk down a long passageway to get into the cinema. Only two of us had money, so they stood shoulder to shoulder at the box office paying for their tickets. Meanwhile the rest of us ran at the double down the passageway and dodged into the cinema. I spent the rest of the afternoon thinking the usherettes were looking for us. The penny finally dropped and we realized that they were only showing people to their seats.

Mrs Barbara Lea

The Hippodrome

The Hippodrome was in Corporation Street, at the other side of what is now Armentieres Square. We didn't go there a lot, but we did go. They had pictures and halfway through they had a turn, somebody singing or doing things like that. We never went upstairs; it were 3d upstairs, but my mother would never let us go upstairs. It were 6d downstairs and we never got in the circle.

Mrs May Redford

Saturday afternoon at the Hippodrome

As children, we used to go to the Hippodrome, to the Saturday afternoon matinée. I think it was only a halfpenny to go in, and we used to have a halfpenny to spend. I used to go into Stalybridge market and buy a halfpenny's worth of faded fruit from Worsley's stall. He used to give me a bag full of rotten apples. We were in the dark in the pictures and I used to sit there happy as Larry. We saw *Flash Gordon* and cowboy films, *Rin Tin Tin*, *Buck Jones* an' all. Then there was one

– I can't remember the name – mummies coming out of the wall. We used to shout. Then, just at the exciting part, it flashed off. My brother used to buy a halfpenny worth of mint balls. He used to suck them until the mint had gone and then put them back in the bag. When the bag had all been sucked, he used to throw them, in the cinema, in the dark. So, if you had a sticky toffee on your head…! We used to come out of the cinema and, if it had been a cowboy, we all used to gallop home. Oh, and *Zorro*. Remember *Zorro*. Oh, happy days!

Mrs Joyce Hall

It's a long way to Tipperary

The best cinema in Stalybridge was the New Princes. They showed MGM and Twentieth Century Fox pictures. It was slightly dearer to go there than to the others. They were the Hippodrome and the Palace. We used to call them 'the bug huts.' In fact, in the downstairs of the Palace, they used to say you went in on your own and came out with company – the fleas. The Shepperton Club, in Corporation Street, is opposite where the Hippodrome was. That is the place where Jack Judge took a bet that he couldn't write and sing a song in the same day. He took the bet and he wrote 'It's a Long Way to Tipperary' for a half crown bet, and sung it at the Hippodrome, which was then the Grand Theatre, that night. I believe it was 1910 or 1911. The song didn't get popular till the First World War, but that's where he first sang it.

Mr Tom Evans

Going up in the gods

The Hippodrome in Stalybridge had stalls, circle and what we called, in those days, 'the gods.' One Bank Holiday afternoon my mother gave me money to see a George

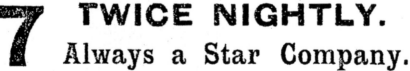

Advertisement for the Hippodrome, Stalybridge, previously the Grand Theatre.

Tel. 156 **PALACE** Stalybridge

COMMENCING JUNE 9th—FOUR DAYS—MON., TUES., WED., and SAT.

BETTY BALFOUR In

"LITTLE DEVIL-MAY-CARE"

NOTE—THURSDAY and FRIDAY ONLY:—

"UNEASY PAYMENTS"

DOMESTIC COMEDY MELODRAMA; Also "FATHER SAID NO."

EVE'S REVIEW—COMEDY.

Advertisement for the Palace cinema, 1928.

Formby film at the Hippodrome. Sad to say, as it was Bank Holiday, there were no half-price seats. Consequently I, along with my friends, didn't have money for full-price tickets. Rather than not see the film, my friends and I decided to go in 'the gods.' This entailed going up a passage by the side of the cinema, climbing up a ladder and going through a square hole at th' top. Then we had to sit on rows of forms. Rather disgruntled at having to 'slum it' like that, we sat on the front form and threw orange peel down on the more affluent members of the audience below.

Mrs Barbara Lea

Auntie Annie, projectionist

Annie Clark was my mother's cousin; in those days anyone who was remotely related to you was your auntie or uncle. She was a projectionist at the Palace for donkey's years, forever. She began as a tea–girl and usherette and worked her way up to being a projectionist. She worked at the Palace more or less all her life. She knew the job inside out; cinema was in her blood.

Mr Ron Watkins

THE END Annie bows out of the picture

My auntie Annie.

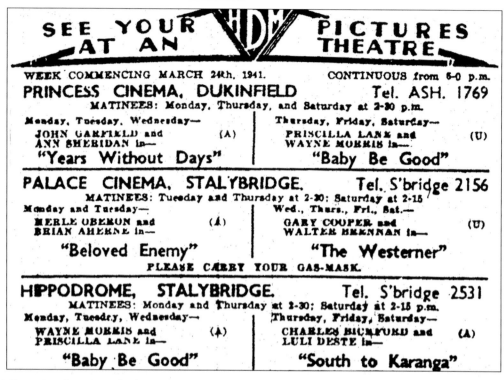

SEE YOUR HDM PICTURES AT AN THEATRE

WEEK COMMENCING MARCH 24th, 1941.   CONTINUOUS from 6-0 p.m.

PRINCESS CINEMA, DUKINFIELD   Tel. ASH. 1769
MATINEES: Monday, Thursday, and Saturday at 2-30 p.m.

Monday, Tuesday, Wednesday—
JOHN GARFIELD and   (A)
ANN SHERIDAN in—
"Years Without Days"

Thursday, Friday, Saturday—
PRISCILLA LANE and   (U)
WAYNE MORRIS in—
"Baby Be Good"

PALACE CINEMA, STALYBRIDGE.   Tel. S'bridge 2156
MATINEES: Tuesday and Thursday at 2-30; Saturday at 2-15

Monday and Tuesday—
MERLE OBERON and   (A)
BRIAN AHERNE in—
"Beloved Enemy"

Wed., Thurs., Fri., Sat.—
GARY COOPER and   (U)
WALTER BRENNAN in—
"The Westerner"

PLEASE CARRY YOUR GAS-MASK.

HIPPODROME, STALYBRIDGE.   Tel. S'bridge 2531
MATINEES: Monday and Thursday at 2-30; Saturday at 2-15 p.m.

Monday, Tuesday, Wednesday—
WAYNE MORRIS and   (A)
PRISCILLA LANE in—
"Baby Be Good"

Thursday, Friday, Saturday—
CHARLES BICKFORD and   (A)
LULI DESTE in—
"South to Karanga"

Composite advertisement for the Princess cinema, Dukinfield, the Palace cinema, Stalybridge, and the Hippodrome cinema, Stalybridge, which all belonged at one time to the HDM circuit.

Dukinfield cinemas

With living on Railway Street when I was younger, we used to go to the Princess a lot. If it was an 'A' film (Adults) we couldn't get in on our own. We used to stand near the Commercial pub at the corner and say to adults, 'Are you going to the pictures? Will you take me in?' We'd all stand there with our tuppence. We used to call the Princess 'The Prinny.' We didn't go to the Oxford an awful lot. They didn't have tickets there; they had a metal disc with a hole in it. When you paid your money, they gave you one of these. It was as big as an old-fashioned shilling but it had a hole in it. The pay-box was at the side in the Oxford, not at the front. The other Dukinfield cinema was the Palladium, on Crescent Road. Dad used to go there a lot. We called it the Palladidlum.

Mrs Alice Edwards

Silent pictures

The Princess, on King Street, was mostly the cinema we went to when we were younger. When we first went it wasn't Talkies, it was silent pictures. At the Saturday matinees they used to have these shoes that came on the screen with a ball bouncing up and down and they had a pianist that played. Any child that went up and would sing got some sweets. There was the Palladium, which was on the corner of Hope Street and Crescent Road. They used to call that 'The Ranch.' It was a little bit of a dump really, showing all these cowboy films. Then they built one on the corner of Oxford Road and Foundry Street. That was the Oxford and it was the first one in Dukinfield to have Talkies. Father loved going to the films and I always went with him. When it was the silent films we went with my mother, because you could take all the children and it didn't matter how much noise they made, because it didn't bother anybody.

Miss Annice Ritson

Two on a seat there!

As a child I used to go to the Princess on a Saturday afternoon. We saw a lot of cowboy things. There used to be a man called Bown, who was the attendant on Saturday afternoons. As the cinema was filling up, he'd come down with a torch. 'Two on a seat there!' he'd shout. We used to try to avoid him. He wanted to make us double up, so he could get more customers in. We didn't like that. The Palladium was on Crescent Road. It had a bit of a low tone, some said. I remember my boss saying to me once, 'Have you heard? They want to turn the Palladium into a swimming baths.' 'I haven't heard that,' I said. 'How do you know that?' 'Well, there's so much breast stroking going on in the back row,' he said.

Mr Fred Travis

Bang! Bang!

I went to the Oxford with Fred a time or two. After Barbara was born, he used to come every week to the Oxford. I think it must have been a cowboy every week, because he used to open the front door and poke his head round the kitchen door and say, 'Bang! Bang!' I'd say, 'Oh, no! Not another cowboy!' He loved them, of course.

Mrs Joyce Travis

Uncle Albert, the chucker-out

I remember the Princess Cinema being built; I was about nine or ten. There weren't individual seats; they were long forms. My uncle Albert was the chucker-out. He used to be there, 'Move up! We've got to get some more in. Come on, move up!' They'd gradually move and he'd have them all stacked up. We never got any concessions, although he was my uncle. Miserable old cove he was! Mind you, it was only a penny for Saturday afternoon. If you'd a lot of money and you could afford tuppence, you could go upstairs. It was as thrilling as anything. There was a piano in the corner. There'd be hundreds of children, all jabbering away. You could never keep them quiet. All at once there'd be a yell because that little white spot would come on the screen to show they were nearly ready to start.

Mr David Cooper

The Palladium

The Palladium was owned by a Mr Taylor and, when he died, his daughter became the owner. My dad was the chief projectionist there. There used to be two projectionists. You didn't have to go into the Palladium to get into the projection box. You went up some steps outside, into this little room where they had the projectors. I used to go on a Saturday afternoon. It was children's day and my dad used to go on the stage. All these kids used to have presents, sweets in tiny cartons and twisted papers and little bits of odds and ends; I don't know what they did for this. I used to sneak into the cinema; never paid; I used to say, 'I'll just go in and see me dad.' The Palladium was about the same size as the Princess down in Dukinfield. You went in at the front; there were glass doors. The pay box was in the middle and the stairs to go up to the balcony were on the right-hand side. It wasn't very big inside. It had beautiful curtains. The balcony went straight across; no side bits. There was one big chandelier. Me dad once fell from the top to the bottom

PALLADIUM, DUKINFIELD Tel. Ash. 1335

Monday to Saturday, Continuous from 6 p.m. Children's Sat. Matinee 2-15.

Oct. 6th—Mon., Tues., Wed.: Thursday, Friday, Saturday:

Lloyd Nolan, Joan Bennett, and Francis Lederer in— Kenny Baker and Frances Langford in—

'The Man I Married' Hit Parade of 1941'

Advertisement for the Palladium, Dukinfield, 1941.

PALLADIUM, DUKINFIELD, *Tel. Ash. 1335*

Mon. to Fri. Cont. 6—10 p.m.; Sat., 2 houses, 6-9 and 8-15. Children's Sat. Mat. 2-15

MAY 19th—MON., TUES., WED.: THURSDAY, FRIDAY, SATURDAY—

JANE WITHERS, GENE AUTRY in— SIDNEY TOLER in

'SHOOTING HIGH" "CHARLIE CHAN'S

Also JON HALL in— MURDER CRUISE"

"SAILOR'S LADY" Also "PONY POST."

Advertisement for the Palladium, which shows its reliance on cowboy pictures.

when he was doing something to the chandelier. We thought he were dead, but he caught hold of the balcony on his way down. The Palladium used to show what I would call second-class movies. They didn't have *Gone With the Wind* or any of the big films. They showed mainly the Three Stooges and things like that. The front of the Palladium opened on Crescent Road and Hope Street was at the side.

Mrs Vera Win Hotchkiss

The Palladium generator

We lived in Zetland Street, which was near the Palladium. They had a generator. You could always tell when they switched it on

because it made a heck of a noise. All night it was whirring away. We'd say, 'The Palladium's switched on now.'

Mr Kenneth Gee

Oh, the Hokey-Cokey!

The Jubilee Hall was wonderful – dances, posh dances, Nalgo dances which went on until two o'clock in the morning. The floor of the Jubilee Hall was sprung, especially for dancing. One time we went in, and heard 'Ladies and gentlemen, before we start, I have to announce there will be no Hokey-Cokey and no Palais Glide. We are ruining the floor.' So we had to do our waltzes and quicksteps and slow foxtrots.

Mrs Ethel Anderson

Richard Whittington

We had an entertainment group, Holy Trinity Entertainment Society. We practised six months for *The Pirates of Penzance*, but we couldn't get enough men in for the chorus and it fell through. When we did *Daddy Longlegs* my wife took the main part of Judy Abbott. I were in it; all I had to say were, 'What's this? Broken cup. She shall be punished'. When we got a new vicar he allowed us to have a pantomime. It were *Dick Whittington*, but he wouldn't let us call it that. We had to call it *Richard Whittington*.

Mr Percy Norton

The May Queen

The biggest thing that ever happened to me, the most special thing was when I became May Queen of Tame Valley in 1951. It was the first Saturday in May. I had to have fresh flowers and a long dress and a crown. It was a big procession. We walked all along Tame Valley, up Sandy Lane, along Foundry Street and King Street. There were children all dressed up, with boxes to collect all the money. And there was a jazz band. Then, in the afternoon, they crowned you. There were nineteen houses on Tame Valley, set back, and they called it the 19 Row. They used to put a platform on there and decorate it with flags. The mayor and other people, who they thought were important, came, and you went up on the platform and got crowned. You had to make a speech. They had a Maypole and all the children danced round the Maypole in front of you while the jazz band played. They usually had a piano on the platform and a soloist. Afterwards you used to go back, usually to the Sunday school and they'd take all the collecting boxes off the children and share out all the money. You used to have to go and queue outside Mrs Greenwood's – I

Mr Ted Owens, who ran the Palladium Cinema, Dukinfield, with his daughter Vera (Win), later Mrs Vera Win Hotchkiss, c. 1937-38.

always remember it being Mrs Greenwood's – and you all got an equal amount. Then, during the year, you had what they called the Tours. This was a big thing, led by the Rose Queens and May Queens. Every few weeks you got to put this dress on again, and your crown and you would have your retinue. A taxi came for you and you went to all the Queens at home.

Mrs Barbara Perry

Jubilee Hall, Dukinfield, with its sprung floor.

Richard *('not Dick')* Whittington. *Holy Trinity,* c. *1934.*

Tame Valley May Queen (now Mrs Barbara Perry) in procession.

Dancing with Dukinfield Operatic Society

As a youngster I went to dancing classes at Mabel Pogson's dancing school at the Conservative Club on Town Lane. Then, when I was sixteen, I joined Dukinfield Operatic Society. I was a dancer. I was in *Chu Chin Chow, Oklahoma, Call Me Madam*. We always put our shows on at the Empire Theatre in Ashton. We rehearsed on a Sunday, when it was getting near the show, at the Jubilee Hall in Dukinfield, in the Lesser Hall. I used to think I was a budding star, but I wasn't. I wasn't a solo dancer. Three of us danced together in one show, and I think I flitted across the stage once.

Mrs Pat Bolt

123

Holy Trinity Centenary Queen (now Mrs Jean Pilling).

Millbrook Rose Queen (now Mrs Margaret Green).

Dukinfield Amateur Operatic Society – Oklahoma.

Dukinfield Amateur Operatic Society – Chu Chin Chow.

Tame Valley Methodist Church pantomime.

Where's the organist?

When they had the May Queen's crowning, they brought a piano out onto the platform and Mr Cook, my piano teacher, used to come and play for me. I was a boy soprano, and I had to go up on the stage and sing. There used to be a girl sung as well. I've always been musical and I started playing the organ at Tame Valley Methodist church when I was thirteen. The congregation were very pleased for me. The lady, who used to play, played hymns slowly. I played them quite a bit faster. I remember one of the congregation saying, 'It was like being in the Grand National'. Not long after I started playing the organ at church, it was a hot night and the sun was streaming through the windows. I was sat at the organ. We used to sing the Lord's Prayer. The sun kept on shining. The preacher gave a long prayer that seemed to go on forever and ever and ever. I nodded off. At that time we had a choir and Mr. Pickering was the conductor. When the preacher said 'Amen', I should have struck up the Lord's Prayer. I was still in noddy-land. Mr Pickering was saying, 'John! John! But no matter how loud he shouted I was still well away. So that night they had to say the Lord's Prayer.

Mr John Perry

Dukinfield cricket team, 1960s.

Old St George's football team, 1935. In the front row, middle, is James Wainwright.

Stalybridge cricket team, 1960s. John Perry is second from left.